# Companion to the Lectionary

## 4. Prayers of Intercession

Christine Odell

# Companion to the Lectionary

## 4. Prayers of Intercession

**EPWORTH PRESS**

British Library Cataloguing in Publication Data

*Companion to the lectionary.
4: Prayers of intercession
1. Public worship
I. Odell, Christine
264    BV10.2*

*ISBN 0–7162–0439–8*

*First published 1987
by Epworth Press,
Room 195, 1 Central Buildings,
Westminster, London SW1H 9NR
Fourth impression 1995*

*Typeset by J & L Composition Ltd
Printed and bound in Great Britain by
Mackays of Chatham PLC, Chatham, Kent*

# Preface

It is a privilege but also a daunting task for any one person to be asked to write intercessory prayers for the whole church year – and especially daunting for someone as inexperienced as I am. I therefore owe a debt of gratitude to all those who supported me as I undertook this challenging exercise.

Thank you!

to Revd Neil Dixon for his reading, appreciation and correction of the typescript. His encouragement and suggestions have been invaluable;

to my parents, Alan and Averil Odell, and to all my family and friends for their interest in the progress of the work and for their loving support;

to the Methodist churches in the Leeds (Headingley) Circuit where some of these prayers have been used and especially to friends in the Cookridge and Adel Methodist churches, who have seen less of their 'minister's wife' than usual;

and most of all to my husband and enabler, Peter Sheasby, who has listened, made suggestions and coffee, gone to the Post Office . . .!

*January 1987*                                          Christine Odell

# Introduction

The practice of intercessory and petitionary prayer is one that begins early in Christian childhood, often with the words 'God bless Mummy and Daddy ... and me', and it is, as such, the simplest form of prayer. Its inherent temptations, however, also make it the most difficult. It sometimes appears that in such prayers we are sending a news bulletin to an omniscient God who knows nothing of what is happening in the world which he has created; or that we are speaking to an all-wise God who needs all the advice he can get on dealing with the problems of sin and suffering!

Prayer has a basic definition of being communication between people and God, between God and people. For such a communication to take place, we need to lay ourselves completely open before God – open in mind and heart and soul. We bring to him all that we are: people with our own needs and anxieties; people who are sons or daughters, husbands or wives, brothers or sisters, parents, friends, colleagues; people who are members of a community, a society; people who are members of Christ's Body, the church; people who are members of the human race. We bring our humanity, with all its shortcomings and sufferings, to God. We bring our home, the world, with all its tensions and imperfections, to God. And, in the name of his Son, Jesus Christ, by whose incarnation we see that God is with us in the midst of an ambiguous world, we pray to God that he may continue his work of loving, healing and redeeming creation. We pray in the confidence that this is so and in gratitude that nothing can separate us from this ever-flowing love; but we pray in order that we may not take it for granted, in order that we may realize it in our own lives and in order that we may ally ourselves with the point of view that God reveals to us in Christ and so become co-workers with him in his plan of salvation.

The prayers in this book contain the elements of both intercessory and petitionary prayer and have been written to be a sharing of ourselves and our experiences, our needs and our concerns, with our loving God.

The accepted liturgical practice today is that, within a service of worship, the prayers of intercession and petition should form part of the Response to the Word as revealed and expounded in scripture reading and sermon. The love that we express in our prayers of intercession is a response to the love of God for us, revealed in the Good News of Jesus Christ.

The title of the theme from the Lectionary is printed above each of the following prayers of intercession in order that they will be found useful not only during the appropriate church service, but also for other services and meetings and for private devotions. It is hoped that these prayers will be used with a fair degree of flexibility, and that worship leaders will feel free to adapt the length and content to the needs of their particular congregation and service.

The words in *italic* print denote congregational participation – in spoken or silent response.

There are spaces left for specific prayers to be made so that, for example, current areas of concern in the news and the names of members of the congregation who are ill may be included.

Any suggestions in brackets are optional.

In most cases, traditional versicles and responses can be substituted for those printed, if desired. A time of silence could also be substituted.

Most of the responses can be easily memorized, if announced clearly a couple of times before prayer begins. If the church has a printed notice sheet, it may be possible to have them printed out.

Many of the prayers would lend themselves to being read out by more than one person. It is recommended that the following should be read by more than one voice:

Second Sunday before Christmas (The Forerunner)
The Watchnight Service
Third Sunday after Easter 1. The Lakeside
Twenty-first Sunday after Pentecost (Endurance)

NB Christmas Day, Midnight Service – there are five verses in this prayer, so that it would be possible to light an Advent candle at the end of each one.

# Ninth Sunday before Christmas
## *(Fifth before Advent)*

### *The Creation*

L: Lord, as members of your creation:
*R: Help us to give as well as to take.*

Let us pray for the world in which we live:
A world rich in resources
Yet exploited and laid waste
By humankind's lack of vision
And lack of respect;
A world of plenty
Where many go hungry;
A world of beauty
Spoilt and sullied;
The planet Earth, our home,
Threatened by total destruction.

Lord, as members of your creation:
*Help us to give as well as to take.*

Let us pray for those with power and influence in the world:
For governments and rulers,
Whose policies pass sentences
Determining the fate of their lands
And those of other countries;
For leaders in industry and commerce;
For those who farm and mine and fish;
For those who seek to make us aware
Of the delicate balances within creation,
Of the need for conservation and care.
(For . . . )

Lord, as members of your creation;
*Help us to give as well as to take.*

## Ninth Sunday before Christmas

Let us pray for the church:
That believing in God, the Father Almighty,
Creator and Sustainer of the world,
We may shoulder our responsibilities
As partners and as stewards.
May we, Lord, by meeting
The challenges of life in your creation,
Reveal you to be
A God of justice, love and wisdom,
The hope of the world.

Lord, as members of your creation:
*Help us to give as well as to take.*

Let us pray for those for whom
Life in the world is very hard
Because of the nature of God's creation,
Or because of our abuse of God's gifts:
For those who hunger or thirst;
For those who are diseased or disabled;
For victims of warfare or disaster.
(For . . . )

Lord, as members of your creation:
*Help us to give as well as to take.*

Let us pray for those
Who find life in God's creation
Meaningless and cruel:
For those who ask 'Why me?';
For those dehumanized by brutality.
Help us to cling to the vision, Lord,
That the world is not designed
To break us, but to make us.
We pray for the redemption of creation,
When the world will see the true glory
Of your love, made known to us in Christ.

In Jesus' name, *Amen.*

# Eighth Sunday before Christmas
*(Fourth before Advent)*

## The Fall

L: Lord, in your mercy:
R: *Hear our prayer.*

We pray for ourselves, Father,
That in the name of your Son
You will deliver us
From our many sins;
From those sins in ourselves
That riddle the whole world,
Coming between us and you,
Threatening to destroy the beauty
Of humankind made in your image.

Lord, in your mercy:
*Hear our prayer.*

Deliver us, Lord, from
The sin of pride;
From setting ourselves above
Other people, and above you.
We pray for those
With power in the world,
That they may know themselves
To be accountable
To you and to your truths,
Wisdom, justice and compassion.
(We pray for . . . )

Lord, in your mercy:
*Hear our prayer.*

Deliver your church, Lord,
From the sin of pride

That shows itself in
Self-righteousness,
Pious words and dogmatism.
In the power of your Spirit
May we become
Humble servants to you
And to the world,
Emptying ourselves, like Christ,
Of all but your love.

Lord, in your mercy:
*Hear our prayer.*

Deliver us, Lord,
From the sin of greed,
From serving ourselves first
And letting others go without.
We pray, Lord, for all those
Who are the victims of our greed;
For those in our society
Who are unable to 'keep up'
In the race for possessions;
For those in other countries
Who hunger or live in strife
Because greedy hands have
Laid hold on their land.

Lord, in your mercy:
*Hear our prayer.*

Deliver your church, Lord,
From the sin of greed;
From forgetting that all we have
Comes from you.
Stop us from hugging to ourselves
Our possessions, our time,
Our talents and our love!
Stop us from hugging to ourselves
Your gospel, your joy,
Your hope and your salvation!

Lord, in your mercy:
*Hear our prayer.*

Deliver us, Lord,
From the sin of despair
That puts a little faith
In ourselves,
And no faith
In you.
In our prayers, Lord,
We ask you to show us where you are
And where we should be.
We pray for all those
Labouring under heavy burdens:
For the sick and bereaved;
For the guilt-ridden and depressed;
For the anxious and the scared.
(For . . . )

Lord, in your mercy,
*Hear our prayer*.

In the name of him who lived and died and was raised, so that the
barriers of sin that we had put between ourselves and God might
be overcome, in the name of Jesus Christ, our Lord and Saviour,
*Amen*.

# Seventh Sunday before Christmas
*(Third before Advent)*

## *The Election of God's People: Abraham*

L: Lord God, we are your people:
*R: Keep us eager and loyal.*

Listen, God is calling us on a journey
Through our lives, and in his world.
He is calling us to be his people
With special tasks and his special help.

Lord God, we are your people:
*Keep us eager and loyal.*

God is calling us to the high places
Where policies and decisions are made.
We must work that in every government
Something of God's kingly rule
May be found.
He is calling us to pray
For the rulers of this world . . .
*(Silence)*

Lord God, we are your people:
*Keep us eager and loyal.*

God is calling us to the low places
Where poverty and suffering reign.
We must work that Christ's brothers and sisters
May be visited and comforted,
Fed and healed and loved,
In his name.
He is calling us to pray
For the needy of this world . . .
*(Silence)*

Lord God, we are your people:
*Keep us eager and loyal.*

God is calling us to dangerous places,
Where sin and temptation abound.
We must work, loving the unlovable,
Forgiving, at terrible cost,
Risking everything for others,
Giving hope.
He is calling us to pray
For the lost in the world . . .
(*Silence*)

Lord, we are your people:
*Keep us eager and loyal.*

God is calling us to holy places,
Places where the church
May find her Lord:
We find him in his world
And in one another;
In the fellowship of worship,
In the quiet of our souls.
God is calling us to work
And to pray
For the whole world.

Lord God, we are your people:
*Keep us eager and loyal.*

In Jesus' name, *Amen*.

# Sixth Sunday before Christmas
*(Second before Advent)*

## *The Promise of Redemption: Moses*

We pray for the Pharoahs of our world today,
For all those who hold others in bondage:
For governments that operate
Cruel and oppressive regimes;
For societies that treat persons
As units for producing wealth;
For families where individuals
Are dominated and not loved;
For those who impose creeds
Of fear and guilt, in God's name.
Loving Father, King of kings,
You did not create us to be slaves
But to be free and to love;
You took responsibility for us
And though we had chosen wrong ways
You sent your Son, Jesus Christ,
To live and die and rise for us.
Grant that the Pharoahs of this world
May take, with their power, responsibility
For every human being in their care.

We pray for those who act as Moses in our world today,
For all who lead struggling peoples from bondage into freedom:
For those who champion the causes
Of the powerless or persecuted;
For those who campaign for human rights
In this and every land;
For those who bring new possibilities
Into the lives of the disabled;
For those who heal those who are sick
In body or in mind;

For those who preach the gospel
Of hope and salvation in Christ.
Loving Father, in Christ we see
The true pattern for all leadership.
As your servant, Moses,
Led the children of Israel
From slavery to freedom
In the Promised Land,
So your Son, Jesus,
Leads your children on
To the kingdom of your love
Where all are whole and free.

Let us pray for all those who are in bondage today,
Whose lives are limited by forces without and fears within:
For those discriminated against,
Persecuted and oppressed;
For the unemployed, and for those
In boring or distasteful jobs;
For those so needed by other people
They have no time to be themselves;
For the housebound, the crippled and the sick;
For those suffering from phobias,
Or feeling unable to cope;
For those dying or bereaved
Who glimpse the bondage of death,
And for ourselves, your people, the church,
Sometimes free, but often found in chains
Of pride and fear and apathy.
Loving Father, Moses was afraid
And the people too, but you provided
Guidance and food and hope.
In Christ you have shown us that
You too were prepared to travel
On the dangerous path of life,
You too shared in the bondage
Of the fears and limitations of humankind.
You relied on the care of others
But were rejected, betrayed and killed,
Yet you rose again to reveal
The glorious liberty of the children of God.
We pray for this vision for the world.

In the name of Christ, our Leader and Saviour, *Amen.*

# Fifth Sunday before Christmas
*(The Sunday before Advent)*

## The Remnant of Israel

L: Lord, hear us:
*R: Lord, graciously hear us.*

Let us pray for our world,
Where might is right
And safety is found in numbers.

Lord, hear us:
*Lord, graciously hear us.*

Let us pray for the church,
God's own people
In a large and sometimes hostile world:
That we may stand
United by love
One in Christ Jesus;
That we may remain
Loyal to our calling
Through every change
   In circumstance,
   In society,
   In thought.

Lord, hear us:
*Lord, graciously hear us.*

Let us pray for the church
Here in . . .
That we may be
Faithful witnesses for God
   To the community,
   To each new generation,
   To each other.

Lord, hear us:
*Lord, graciously hear us.*

Let us pray
For those churches
Whose congregations
Are dwindling,
That the power
Of the Risen Lord
May grant them courage,
Wisdom and hope.

Lord, hear us:
*Lord, graciously hear us.*

Let us pray
For those people
Of other races
Who find themselves
In a minority in this land,
That they might find
Acceptance and welcome,
Yet retain the integrity
Of their identity.

Lord, hear us:
*Lord, graciously hear us.*

Let us pray
For those who battle for
Unpopular causes
In the name of conscience,
Prepared to suffer and die
For truths which live on.

Lord, hear us:
*Lord, graciously hear us.*

Let us pray
That governments may listen
To the voices of individuals
As well as those
Of powerful groups;
Rule by right

And not by might;
Seek to meet
The real needs of all.

Lord, hear us:
*Lord, graciously hear us.*

Let us pray for those
Whom we know who are ill
Or distressed, or in any
Kind of need . . .

Let us pray
That our prayers,
Small and weak
Though they may seem,
May bring us to the side
Of our crucified Lord,
So that the power
Of his love and suffering
May transform us,
The church and the world.

Lord, hear us:
*Lord, graciously hear us. Amen.*

# Fourth Sunday before Christmas
## (Advent 1)

### The Advent Hope

L: To a world in need of hope:
R: Come, Lord, come!

Lord, we are appalled
By the news we read and hear.
We are appalled
By the injustice in your world.
We see:
The powerful ranged against the powerless;
The greedy exploiting the needy;
The clever using the simple;
The evil inflicting suffering on the innocent.

Everywhere we look we see injustice:
    in families;
    in communities;
    in the church;
    in society;
    between nations.

We are human and limited; and our judgement is
Our blinkered sight               distorted
Distorts our judgment
Between wrong and right.
But you, Lord, you know
The reality of things;
The real needs and motives
Hidden deep within us.
We ask that your judgment
May enlighten the world,
So that leaders and people
May strive for your justice.

## Fourth Sunday before Christmas

To a world in need of hope:
*Come, Lord, come!*

Lord, we are wearied
By the news we read and hear.
We are wearied
By the folly in your world.
We see:
Entertainment preferred to the tackling of serious issues;
Prosperity preferred to the search for real life;
Short term measures preferred to long term planning;
Independence preferred to the give and take of love.

Everywhere we look we see folly:
    in our own values;
    in the conduct of the church;
    in the attitudes of society;
    in politics at home and abroad.

We are human and limited
By the superficial nature
Of our understanding
But you, Lord, you
Are wisdom and knowledge.
You see what was, what is
And what will be.
We ask that your wisdom
May inform the world,
So that leaders and people
May move forward together.

To a world in need of hope:
*Come, Lord, come!*

Lord, we are frightened
By the news we read and hear.
We are frightened
By the conflict in your world.
We see:
~~The threat of nuclear war;~~ Everywhere we look we see violence
The quick recourse to violence;
Wars between creed and creed, ~~race and race, nation and nation;~~
People in turmoil within themselves.

Everywhere we look we see violence:
 in homes;
 on our television screens;
 in our streets;
 in every land.

We are human and limited;
Our fear of loss of self
Makes us aggressive and unkind
But you, Lord, you
Are the Prince of Peace.
In Christ you gave yourself
That we might be one
With ourselves, other people and you.
We ask that your peace
May inspire the world;
That leaders and people may find
Joy in togetherness of life.

To a world in need of hope;
*Come, Lord, come!*

Lord, we need to hear
Good news, your Good News
Brought to us in Christ;
The news that you
Are at work in the world,
The news that
Your Name is Love.

To a world in need of hope:
*Come, Lord, come! Amen.*

# Third Sunday before Christmas
*(Advent 2)*

## *The Word of God in the Old Testament*

L: Lord, in your mercy:
*R: Hear our prayer.*

> Word of God
> Creating the world
> 'Let there be light'
> Word of action.

We pray for those
Whose words will lead to actions:
For governments, whose discussions
Determine the future of their lands;
For those in authority, whose words
Are words that command and control;
For meetings at our church
Where decisions have to be made;
For people debating in their minds
About what they should do next.

Lord, in your mercy:
*Hear our prayer.*

> Word of God
> Showing God to us
> 'I am what I am'
> Word of revelation.

We pray for those
Whose words lead others to understanding:
For all who spread your gospel
And translate its words and thoughts;
For teachers at school or college

And those in Junior Church (or Sunday School);
For journalists and broadcasters
Who tell us more of your world.

Lord, in your mercy:
*Hear our prayer.*

> Word of God
> Feeding hungry souls
> With spiritual manna
> Word of life.

We pray for those
Whose words feed other people:
For authors and poets whose words
Feed people hungry for beauty;
For charities who raise money
To feed and clothe and educate;
For ourselves, as we try to meet
The deep needs and hungers of others.

Lord, in your mercy:
*Hear our prayer.*

> Word of God
> Embracing his world
> 'Comfort, comfort my people'
> Word of concern.

We pray for those
Whose words comfort other people:
For those who counsel and listen to
The depressed and afraid;
For those working in hospices and hospitals
Who care for the sick and the dying;
For all those engaged in pastoral work
From within the community of this church;
For ourselves, that we may find
The right words and the right silences.

Lord, in your mercy:
*Hear our prayer.*

> Word of God
> Speaking forgiveness
> Healing the broken
> Word of love.

## Third Sunday before Christmas

We pray for those
Who need to find words of love:
For families split apart
By jealousy and disagreement;
For husbands and wives,
Friends and companions,
Who take one another for granted;
For those who care for children
Who feel unwanted and insecure;
For ourselves, as we try
To follow Christ in the world.

Lord, in your mercy:
*Hear our prayer. Amen.*

# Second Sunday before Christmas
*(Advent 3)*

## *The Forerunner*

> 'There is nothing that will stop me speaking out against government oppression – whatever form it takes. The powerless have no voice, so those of us with speech and beliefs must be the conscience of the nations.'

Lord, as John the Baptist came proclaiming your message of justice, may we, the church, be prophets for our own time. Help us to work to make governments more aware of their responsibilities to those under their authority, whether they are rich or poor, black or white, male or female, and whatever their political or religious persuasion.

(We pray for ... )

We ask that by our words, prayers and actions, we may be forerunners for your kingdom of love, justice and peace.

> 'I can't *make* my child become a Christian – I wish it was that simple. But I hope that what I do and what I say will show what Christ means to me, will show where God may be found.'

Lord, as John the Baptist came to prepare the way for your coming, may we, the church, seek to prepare the way for you to come into the lives of others. Help us so to follow Christ that in all our relationships with other people something of his love may be seen, something of his nature understood.

(We pray for ... )

We ask that by our words, prayers and actions, we may be forerunners for Christ to enter the lives of others.

> 'I'm not sitting in judgment on other people by living in this simple manner – but I don't agree with the way this society is going. For me, quality of life comes from what you are, and not from what you earn.'

## Second Sunday before Christmas

Lord, as John the Baptist came to call the people to repentance, may we, the church, offer to others, by our witness and example, an alternative way of life; a way of life based on love and truth rather than selfishness and complacency. Help us to keep a clear view of your goodness, so that our values may reflect our faith and not the values of the society around us.

(We pray for . . . )

We ask that by our words, prayers and actions, we may be forerunners for the salvation of humankind.

> 'Is everyone in church happily married, perfectly adjusted, certain of their faith, totally respectable? Or do they just believe they should appear to be? Is there room for a mixed up sinner like me?'

Lord, as John the Baptist came to challenge the religious people of his day, may we, the church, always be ready to challenge our own attitudes and traditions in the name of love. Help our church to become a place of healing where the anxious and depressed, the sick and bereaved, and those who believe they are of little worth, may find acceptance and love.

(We pray for those for whom we feel particular concern . . . )

We ask that by our words, prayers and actions, we may be forerunners for the joy of life in Christ. *Amen.*

# The Sunday before Christmas
## (Advent 4)

## The Annunciation

L: We, ~~like Mary~~, have a challenge from you:
R: ~~Help us to say 'Yes'~~. Help us, our Father.

Loving, heavenly Father, you call us so that through us your will
might be done on earth. You ask us, weak and blind and imperfect
as we are, to help you to transform the world by love. You
challenge us to say 'yes' to you and to your ~~demands~~ will.

We, ~~like Mary~~, have a challenge from you:
*Help us ~~to say~~ 'Yes'.*

Lord, we pray in love for the people we know, for our families, our
friends and neighbours, and for our sisters and brothers in the
church here in ... We pray for those who are ill, or in any kind of
need or difficulty, thinking especially of ...

*Silence*

Lord, you challenge us to show your love in our love for one
another. May we accept that challenge by sharing in the joys and
sorrows of those around us and by caring for and comforting those
in need.

We, ~~like Mary~~, have a challenge from you:
*Help us ~~to say 'Yes'~~.*

Lord, we pray in love for our community and for the country in
which we live. We pray for all those who work to serve the people
of this land:
   for our government and for the Royal Family;
   for those who provide us with food;
   for those who provide us with necessities and luxuries;
   for those who work to produce energy:
   for those who work for the welfare of the state – social workers,
      doctors and nurses;

for those who keep order in our society – the police force and
the legal profession;
for those who entertain and inform us;
for teachers, lecturers and researchers;
for charity workers and for ministers;
for . . .

*Silence*

Lord, you challenge us to serve you in our daily lives. May we
accept that challenge and in all our occupations, at work or at
home, may we be inspired by your spirit to live lives of selflessness,
thoughtfulness and love.

We, like Mary, have a challenge from you:
*Help us to say 'Yes'.*

We pray, in love, for the many people in the world whom we do
not know, who are suffering or anxious:
for the hungry, the thirsty, the homeless;
for the victims of warfare, accident or natural disaster;
for those who are sick in body, mind or personality;
for the persecuted, the imprisoned and the tortured;
for the lonely, the abandoned and bereaved;
for . . .

*Silence*

Lord, you challenge us to action in a world where your love and
justice are often hard to find. May we accept that challenge and
work together, inspired by the vision of your kingdom of joy and
peace.

We, like Mary, have a challenge from you:
*Help us to say 'Yes'.* Our Father

We pray, in love, for your handmaid, the church, for Christians
everywhere and for ourselves:
that our commitment to Christ the Way may be more than
lukewarm;
that our faith in God alone may enable us to face all challenges;
that we may be inspired by the Holy Spirit and bound together
with love;
that we may be eager to serve and find fulfilment in our calling.

We, like Mary, have a challenge from you:
*Help us to say 'Yes'.*

Lord, we give thanks to you for all those who, through the ages, have said 'Yes' to your love and your commands. We pray that we may follow their example and come with them into your kingdom of joy, where the whole of your creation will be united in one glorious shout of 'Yes' to you.

In the name of him who said 'Yes' so that we might know our Father God, our Lord and Saviour, Jesus Christ, *Amen*.

# Christmas Day

## Midnight

L: The Lord hears our prayer:
*R: Thanks be to God.*

It is dark.
The world is covered in darkness,
The darkness of fear:
Fear of war, of rumours of war;
Fear of violence;
Fear of total destruction;
Fear of the demands of love;
Fear of death.
Lord, we pray for this dark world.

Look, the Light of the World is come!

The Lord hears our prayer:
*Thanks be to God.*

It is dark.
The world is covered in darkness,
The darkness of inhumanity:
Inhumanity leading to persecution;
Inhumanity leading to oppression;
Inhumanity leading to injustice;
Inhumanity leading to exploitation;
Inhumanity betraying the high calling of humankind.
Lord, we pray for this dark world.

Look, the Light of the World is come!

The Lord hears our prayer:
*Thanks be to God.*

It is dark.
The world is covered in darkness,
The darkness of ignorance:
Ignorance resulting in prejudice;
Ignorance resulting in disease;
Ignorance resulting in false confidence;
Ignorance resulting in error;
Ignorance that does not know itself.
Lord, we pray for this dark world.

Look, the Light of the World is come!

The Lord hears our prayer:
*Thanks be to God.*

It is dark.
The world is covered in darkness,
The darkness of suffering:
Suffering from hunger or thirst;
Suffering from illness or disability;
Suffering from depression or anxiety;
Suffering from cruelty or neglect;
Suffering from lack of love;
Suffering from loving.
Lord, we pray for this dark world.

Look, the Light of the World is come!

The Lord hears our prayer:
*Thanks be to God.*

It is dark.
The world is covered in darkness,
The darkness of despair:
Despair about the future of the earth;
Despair about society;
Despair about our own weaknesses;
Despair about suffering;
Despair that daylight will never come.
Lord, we pray for this dark world.

Look, the Light of the World is come!

The Lord hears our prayer:
*Thanks be to God.*

In the name of Jesus Christ, *Amen*.

# Christmas Day

## The Birth of Christ

L: Lord Christ, Baby Jesus:
R: *Welcome to your world!*

Thank you for coming, Lord,
As a helpless baby,
To a world where people try to ignore
The responsibility they have for one another.
We pray for those who feel unloved
Because they are lonely or rejected.
(For ... )

Thank you for coming, Lord,
As a helpless baby,
To show us God himself can be found
In meeting the needs of other people.

Lord Christ, Baby Jesus:
*Welcome to your world!*

Thank you for coming, Lord,
King of kings,
To a world whose leaders and whose rulers
Often use their power unwisely and unwell.
We pray for all countries where
The people suffer from injustice,
From persecution or oppression;
(For ... )

Thank you for coming, Lord,
King of kings,
To give us a vision of the kingdom of God,
Where love, justice and mercy prevail.

Lord Christ, Baby Jesus:
*Welcome to your world.*

Thank you for coming, Lord,
Homeless and poor,
To a world where many
Spend lifetimes of suffering,
Their existence defined
By the search for food.
We pray for all those in need or difficulty,
For the destitute, the hungry and the sick;
(For . . . )

Thank you for coming, Lord,
Homeless and poor,
That in our suffering and anxiety
We may be sure
That God understands
And is with us.

Lord Christ, Baby Jesus:
*Welcome to your world!*

Thank you for coming, Lord,
Saviour and God,
To a world where people put all their faith
In themselves, their achievements and possessions.
We pray for those who find life joyless and empty,
Who escape into a haze of drugs or alcohol,
Or keep too busy to leave time to think;
(For . . . )

Thank you for coming, Lord,
Saviour and God,
To bring us the message of forgiveness and hope,
The promise of a new, rich life in you.

Lord Christ, Baby Jesus:
*Welcome to your world!*

In the name of Immanuel, God with us, *Amen*.

# The Sunday after Christmas

## *The Wise Men*

Lord, in our prayers we offer to you
The gold, frankincense and myrrh of our world.

    Gold.
    The gold of kings.
    The gold that buys
    Power to rule lives.
    The gold that buys
    Things of beauty.
    The gold that buys
    Weapons of destruction.
    The gold that buys
    Food and health and education.
    The gold that buys
    More poverty for the poor.
    The gold that buys
    The conscience of a nation
    Of its leaders and its people.

    We pray:
       for those who own money;
       for those who use it;
       for those who are without it.
Lord, we lay the gold of the world at your feet.

    Frankincense.
    Incense of worship
    By the people of God.
    A people called
    To spread the sweetness of the gospel.
    A people called
    But finding faith hard.
    A people called

To serve the sick and needy.
A people called
But afraid to love.
A people called
To be a fragrant, living sacrifice.
A people called
Whose senses are dulled
Through lack of prayer.

We pray:
    for the church of God;
    for its ministers and leaders;
    for its people worldwide.
Lord, we lay the frankincense of the world at your feet.

Myrrh.
Herb of death,
Death fulfilling suffering.
Suffering from neglect,
From cold or hunger.
Suffering from pain,
From illness or injury.
Suffering from sorrow,
Bereavement or depression.
Suffering from fear,
Anxiety or loneliness.
Suffering from prejudice,
Oppression or war.

We pray:
    for the suffering;
    for the dying;
    for those who care for them.
Lord, we lay the myrrh of the world at your feet.

Take our gold, frankincense and myrrh, our wealth, worship and lives, and use them in your service, in the name of Jesus Christ of Bethlehem. *Amen.*

# Second Sunday after Christmas

## 1. The Presentation in the Temple

L: Lord, in your love we have hope:
R: *Make us messengers of hope for the world.*

Lord, the peoples of the world are waiting:  + long
    They are waiting for peace;
    They are waiting for justice;
    They are waiting for the overthrow of tyranny;
    They are waiting for human rights;
    They are waiting for education.
    They wait:
        for the rains to come;
        for harvest-time;
        for medical care;
        for the next food parcel;
        for the warmth of the day.
The peoples of the world are waiting.

Lord, in your love we have hope:
*Make us messengers of hope for the world.*

Lord, the governments of the world are waiting:
    They are waiting for the rich
    To show concern for the poor
    Before they act
    To alleviate poverty;
    They are waiting for other governments
    To give up nuclear arms
    Before they declare
    Their own disarmament;
    They are waiting until all
    Think as they think
    Before granting free speech;
    They are waiting until

They feel secure
Before putting an end
To torture and oppression.
The governments of the world are waiting.

Lord, in your love we have hope:
*Make us messengers of hope for the world.*

Lord, your church is waiting:
　We are waiting for new life;　+ long
　We are waiting for people to turn to you;
　We are waiting for fresh calls to service;
　We are waiting for a new vision and deeper unity;
　We are waiting for the coming of your kingdom.
　We are waiting:
　　sometimes impatiently;
　　sometimes despairingly;
　　sometimes in apathy;
　　sometimes in confusion.
Lord, we, your church, are waiting.

Lord, in your love we have hope:
*Make us messengers of hope for the world.*

Lord, we pray for those who are waiting for the resolution of their
difficulties:　+ longer
　for the ill who wait for healing;
　for the dying who wait for death;
　for the anxious who wait for time to pass;
　for the prisoners who wait for release;
　for the bereaved who wait for the shedding of tears;
　for the lonely who wait for others to come;
　for the depressed who wait for hope;
　for the unemployed who wait for a job;
　for all those who wait for forgiveness.

We pray for those we know in any kind of need . . .

Lord, in your love we have hope:
*Make us messengers of hope for the world.*

In Jesus' name, *Amen.*

# Second Sunday after Christmas

## 2. The Visit to Jerusalem

L: Lord, if we lose sight of you:
R: *Call and show us where you are.*

The world is such a busy place, Lord:
 Governments are busy,
 dealing with so many issues
 that some have to get pushed aside.
 People are busy,
 making a living,
 meeting together,
 enjoying themselves.
 The church is busy
 with meetings and groups,
 with causes and with visiting.
 We are busy,
 and our thoughts dart hither and thither,
 into the past and into the future.

Lord, if we lose sight of you:
*Call and show us where you are.*

The world is such an anxious place, Lord:
 Governments are anxious
 about the future of their lands,
 about decisions they have to take.
 People are anxious,
 worried about themselves
 and the people they love.
 The church is anxious
 when its attendance falls,
 when commitment seems weak.

*Lord we pray for those who are anxious*

We are anxious
and our responsibilities
are a heavy burden on us.

Lord, if we lose sight of you:
*Call and show us where you are.*

The world is such a needy place, Lord:
Governments are needy –
they never have enough money
to fulfil all their commitments.
People are needy –
they starve for food, for shelter,
for a sense of purpose, for love.
The church is needy
because sometimes she is too timid
to avail herself of the Bread of Life.
We are needy
because we do not really understand
our own needs, or those of others.

Lord, if we lose sight of you:
*Call and show us where you are.*

The world is a place of such suffering, Lord:
Governments are suffering
as a result of their own mistakes
or because of errors in the past.
People are suffering,
they are sick in body or mind,
they have lost people they love.
The church is suffering
alongside the suffering of the world
and because of persecution.
We are suffering,
torn apart by conflicting emotions,
with little peace in ourselves.

Lord, when we lose sight of you:
*Call and show us where you are.*

In the name of Jesus Christ, who came to bring us peace and
wisdom, succour and healing, *Amen.*

# Epiphany

L: Lord, in your mercy:
R: *Hear our prayer.*

We ask, O Lord, that the world may be given the wisdom of
the wise men.

The wise men had the wisdom to be guided by you.

We pray that the rulers of this world may be guided by your
principles of justice, compassion and mercy.

We pray that the church may keep a listening ear to hear your
Word in new and different situations.

We pray that the people of the world may come to understand that
their humanity is made whole in you.

Lord, in your mercy:
*Hear our prayer.*

The wise men had the wisdom to undertake an arduous
journey in search of the truth.

We pray that the rulers of the world may strenuously seek the best
for all their people.

We pray that the church may take up her cross and follow in the
footsteps of Christ her Lord.

We pray that the people of the world may work and struggle
together for the rights of humankind.

Lord, in your mercy:
*Hear our prayer.*

The wise men had the wisdom to inquire diligently about the
facts.

34

We pray that the rulers *people* of the world may make the right use of knowledge in their decision-making. *+ key*

We pray that the church may, by study and debate, ~~contribute to~~ the thought of this modern age. *challenge + shape*

~~We pray that the peoples of the world may~~ be freed by education from the superstition, fear and prejudice of ignorance.

> Lord, in your mercy:
> *Hear our prayer*.

> The wise men had the wisdom to see God in a helpless child.

We pray that the rulers *+ people* of the world may look to the interests of the powerless under their protection.

We pray that the church may be a sanctuary and a support for the poor, the down-trodden and the rejected.

~~We pray that the peoples of the world may come to respect one *+ to see one* another as the equal children of God.~~ *as made equally noble in your image.*

> Lord, in your mercy:
> *Hear our prayer*.

> The wise men had the wisdom to worship the revealed glory of God.

We pray that the rulers of the world may govern in accordance with a vision of goodness and truth.

We pray for the church, that she may find the worship of God food and drink for her life.

We pray that the peoples of the world may find beauty and joy and peace in their lives.

> Lord, in your mercy:
> *Hear our prayer*.

> The wise men had the wisdom to protect the good they had found.

We pray that the rulers of the world may protect and listen to those who champion morality in their land.

We pray that churches may encourage and support their members through times of conflict and doubt.

*who speak out + protect goodness + truth*

## Epiphany

We pray that the people of the world may not be overcome with cynicism, but see what is of value in one another.

> Lord, in your mercy:
> *Hear our prayer*.

Lord, the wisdom of your gospel often seems foolishness to those who do not believe. Help us so to work for your kingdom of love and truth and peace that the world may see and understand.

In Jesus' name, *Amen*.

*a knowledge of you in theory*

# First Sunday after Epiphany

## The Baptism of Christ

L: Lord, this is our prayer:
*R: Help us to know and to do your will.*

Loving Father,
Through Christ your Son
We have become
Your sons and daughters.
We pray for the church,
That we might live up to our calling
As your children;
By loving and accepting one another;
By living in faithfulness to you;
By serving you in the world.
We pray for those
Baptized into your church
From within this community:
That they may follow you all their lives;
That we, by our words, prayers and example,
May show them the love and joy of faith.

Lord, this is our prayer:
*Help us to know and to do your will.*

Loving Father,
Through Christ your Son
We have become
Your sons and daughters.
We pray for those of your children who
Are treated as less than human:
They are oppressed and exploited;
They are imprisoned for their beliefs;
They are discriminated against;
They are used to make money and

Used to fight wars.
We pray for those with power and influence
That they may seek dignity and freedom,
Justice and the opportunity for happiness
For their fellow human beings.

Lord, this is our prayer:
*Help us to know and to do your will.*

Loving Father,
Through Christ your Son
We have become
Your sons and daughters.
We pray for those of our brothers and sisters
Who are suffering or in any kind of distress:
For the hungry and the malnourished;
For the homeless and for refugees;
For the ill and the dying;
For the anxious and depressed;
For those filled with guilt or regret;
For those handicapped in mind or body.
We pray, Lord, that your Spirit may guide
Those who seek to help, to heal and to comfort.

Lord, this is our prayer:
*Help us to know and to do your will.*

Loving Father,
Through Christ your Son
We have become
Your sons and daughters.
At baptism we are called to follow Christ
In the church and out into the world.
We pray for ourselves
For we are tossed by temptation and doubt
About what you want us to do.
We pray that in obedience to you
We may discover the right tasks for us
And serve you with heart and soul and mind.
We pray that in joy we may work together
For the coming of your kingdom of love.

Lord, this is our prayer:
*Help us to know and to do your will.*

In the name of Jesus Christ your Son, our Brother and our
Saviour, *Amen.*

# Second Sunday after Epiphany

## *The First Disciples*

Jesus says,
    'Leave your nets,
    Come, follow me!'

People of the world,
Leave your nets!
Leave behind those ways of living
That stop you following Christ!
Leave behind your obsessions
    with money
    with pleasure
    with escapism
    with popularity
    with self
And come follow him into True Life,
Where you will find
    riches in poverty
    joy in suffering
    peace in facing up to reality
    acceptance in facing up to weakness
    love through self-giving.
Lord, we pray that the people of the world may leave their nets
and follow you.

Governments of the world,
Leave your nets!
Leave behind those ways of governing
That stop you following Christ!
Leave behind your weapons
    of oppression
    of exploitation
    of injustice

    of persecution
    of armed conflict
And come, follow him into the Kingdom of God
Where you will find
    true liberty
    human dignity
    justice
    equality
    peace.
Lord, we pray that the governments of the world may leave their nets and follow you.

Christ's bride, the church,
Leave your nets.
Leave behind those narrow concerns
That stop you following Christ.
Leave behind your blinkers of
    self-righteousness
    respectability
    exclusiveness
    dogmatism
    fear of the world.
Come, follow him in the power of the Spirit:
    forgiven and thankful
    humble and confident
    valued and loving
    a pilgrim people
    of courage and hope,
    travelling on together
    united in God's love.
Lord, we pray that all Christians may leave their nets and follow you.

We pray, Lord, for those whose lives are ensnared within the limitations caused by sickness or by hunger. We pray, too, for those who can see no way out of the suffering in their lives – for the depressed, the bereaved and the anxious. (We pray for those whom we know who are finding life hard and frustrating . . .) We ask that they, reassured by your presence and uplifted by our care and concern, may find true freedom and hope.

We make our prayers in the name of him who calls us to follow, Jesus Christ, our Lord and Saviour. *Amen.*

# Third Sunday after Epiphany

*The First Sign: 1. The Wedding at Cana*

L: Lord Jesus, turn the water of our lives
*R: Into the wine of your kingdom.*

Lord, we need water
But it can seem dull and tasteless.
We need governments
    to keep order
    to structure society
    to protect the weak
    to curb the strong
But, Lord, we pray
That governments may look beyond
The water of their duties
And seek to promote
Quality of life
For all their peoples:
Freedom and justice and peace.

Lord Jesus, turn the water of our lives
*Into the wine of your kingdom.*

Lord, we need water
But it can seem dull and tasteless.
We need the church because
We need each other and you
But sometimes our Christian life together
Lacks the sparkle and colour of good wine.
We pray, Lord, that the church
May be disturbed by your Spirit,
Bringing challenge and excitement and worship,
New thoughts, new words and new rhythms,
Pushing and pulling us into adventurous life.

Lord Jesus, turn the water of our lives
*Into the wine of your kingdom.*

Lord, we need water
But it can seem dull and tasteless.
We pray for those whose lives
Are dulled by monotony and struggle;
Those suffering from:
      hunger
      illness
      depression
      boredom
      loneliness
      bereavement.
We pray that their lives may be transformed by the knowledge of
your presence, through the love of other people.

Lord Jesus, turn the water of our lives
*Into the wine of your kingdom.*

In the name of Jesus, the Bridegroom of his people, *Amen*.

# Third Sunday after Epiphany

## 2. *The New Temple*

L: Lord, the temple of your world is corrupted:
*R: Cleanse it with your love.*

Lord God, you created
Order out of chaos,
For ~~humankind needs order~~ we need order
To live and grow,
But the governments of the world
Have exploited that need;
Some have tyrannized their people,
Ruled with injustice and violence, or gained wealth
~~Others have seduced their people~~
~~With wealth gained~~ from exploitation:
All fall short
Of your standards
Of wisdom, mercy and compassion.

Lord, the temple of your world is corrupted:
*Cleanse it with your love.*

Lord God, you designed
The world to be our home,
A place to live and to learn,
Of challenge and opportunity;
But we are appalled and depressed
By the suffering in the world:
By illness and deformities;
By disasters and accidents;
By hunger and thirst and homelessness;
By death and bereavement.
We find the way hard,

For others as much as for ourselves,
But we trust in your plan
Of redemption.

Lord, the temple of your world is corrupted:
*Cleanse it with your love.*

Lord God, you created ~~us~~ us
~~The family of humankind~~
To love and serve ~~one another~~; you
To love and serve ~~you;~~ one andher
But we have ignored your voice
And lived in selfishness and greed
So that the world is full of evil:
Of hunger for food and for love;
Of prejudice and intolerance;
Of warfare and mindless violence;
~~Of children neglected and abused.~~
~~This darkness tries to quench~~
~~The light of the human spirit~~
Kindled by you.
    our lives
Lord, the temple of your world is corrupted:
*Cleanse it with your love.*

Lord God, you have ~~chosen~~ made us to seek after you
~~To make humankind religious:~~
The church's faith and worship
Is a centre for our lives.
But we often hold the church back
From showing your love to the world
By making it exclusive and daunting;
~~By loading people down with heavy guilt;~~
By being ~~far~~ too inward looking;
By being dogmatic and narrow-minded.
~~We put our faith in religiosity~~    help us to understand your unbound
~~And try to forget~~    love to us so that we may show
~~Our suffering, self-giving Lord.~~    love to the world
           our church
Lord, the temple of ~~your world~~ is corrupted:
*Cleanse it with your love.*

Lord, you bring judgment into our lives, but with it comes the
promise of forgiveness and the hope of joy. We pray for the temple
of the world that it may ~~become~~ a place consecrated to you. *Amen.*
    of our lives, of our church.

45

# Fourth Sunday after Epiphany

## 1. The Friend of Sinners

L: Lord, in your mercy:
R: *Hear our prayer.*

Lord, we bring before you those whom our society condemns as sinners:
    we pray for the man imprisoned for a crime that even his fellow prisoners condemn;
    we pray for the woman imprisoned for pushing drugs in order to feed her own habit;
    we pray for the boy who has mugged a frail old lady and left her alone and injured;
    we pray for the girl who has vandalized property and daubed obscenities on our walls.

We pray for all those who have given in to their worst impulses of greed, hatred, lust or violence.

Jesus, friend of sinners, help us to find the right ways of loving those whom our society condemns as sinners.

*Silence*

Lord, in your mercy:
*Hear our prayer.*

Lord, we bring before you those who hate themselves because of what they are or have done:
    we pray for the man who knocked down a pedestrian and drove away;
    we pray for the woman who cannot stop herself stealing from shops;
    we pray for the boy who quarrelled with his mother just before she died;
    we pray for the girl who sleeps around but longs to feel she can say 'no'.

We pray for all those who are heavily weighed down by feelings of guilt and regret.

Jesus, friend of sinners, help us to find the right ways of loving those who hate themselves.

*Silence*

Lord, in your mercy:
*Hear our prayer*

Lord, we bring ourselves to you, because we fall so far short of what you want us to be:

we pray for the man afraid to follow you, because of what might be asked of him;

we pray for the woman who makes herself indispensable to others, because she thinks she is worth little, even to you;

we pray for the boy who uses his religion to make himself feel superior to those around him;

we pray for the girl who cannot accept that you forgive her, because she cannot forgive herself.

We pray for ourselves, that your Holy Spirit may keep leading us onward, into a life lived closer to you.

Jesus, friend of sinners, help us to find the right ways of loving ourselves and one another.

*Silence*

Lord, in your mercy:
*Hear our prayer. Amen.*

# Fourth Sunday after Epiphany

## 2. *Life for the World*

> L: Lord, hear us:
> *R: Lord, graciously hear us.*

Let us pray:
Jesus came to bring Life for the World.
Let us bring before God in our prayers those things in our world
which result in the destruction of life:

> Warfare　　　　　(in ... )
> (*Silence*)
>
> Starvation　　　　(in ... )
> (*Silence*)
>
> Disease　　　　　(in ... )
> (*Silence*)
>
> Disaster　　　　　(in ... )
> (*Silence*)
>
> Lord, hear us:
> *Lord, graciously hear us.*

Jesus came to bring Life for the World.
Let us bring before God in our prayers those things in our world
which deny the value of every person's life:

> Injustice　　　　　(in ... )
> (*Silence*)
>
> Discrimination　　(on the grounds of ... )
> (*Silence*)
>
> Exploitation　　　(by ... )
> (*Silence*)

Oppression        (by . . . )
(*Silence*)

Lord, hear us:
*Lord, graciously hear us.*

Jesus came to bring Life for the World.
Let us bring before God in our prayers those people in our society
who may be finding life empty:

The prisoner     ( . . . )
(*Silence*)

The unemployed ( . . . )
(*Silence*)

The addict       ( . . . )
(*Silence*)

The lonely       ( . . . )
(*Silence*)

Lord, hear us:
*Lord, graciously hear us.*

Jesus came to bring Life for the World.
Let us bring before God in our prayers those people we know who
are finding everyday life a struggle:

The ill           (for . . . )
(*Silence*)

The bereaved   (for . . . )
(*Silence*)

The sad        (for . . . )
(*Silence*)

The anxious    (for . . . )
(*Silence*)

Lord, hear us:
*Lord, graciously hear us.*

We thank you, Lord, for your gift of abundant life.
We pray that the church, being filled with your Spirit and united in
your love, may witness to the world the joy, richness and
satisfaction of life lived in Christ.

We make our prayers in the Saviour's name, *Amen.*

# Fifth Sunday after Epiphany

## 1. The New Dispensation

L: Lord, this is our prayer:
*R: Help us to know and to do your will.*

Heavenly Father,
You have sent us your Son
To make all things new;
We have, in your Spirit,
A new relationship with you,
A new way of seeing,
a new way of life.

With new eyes we look
At the world around us
And see the old ways re-enacted
Time after time after time:
The tyranny of the powerful;
The greed of the wealthy;
Injustice, cruelty and aggression.
But we also see
God's Spirit at work,
Disturbing the dirt of ages,
Challenging, stirring people up;
And we pray
For that new, clean world
To which he calls us on,
Where lands are ruled with wisdom,
Justice and mercy and compassion;
Where honesty lays open
The thoughts of those in power.

Lord, this is our prayer:
*Help us to know and to do your will.*

With new eyes we look
At the faces of the people of the world
And we see those age-old expressions
That haunt humankind:
The gaunt, listless look
Of the hungry, naked child;
The lines of pain and suffering
On the faces of the sick;
The startled, nervous twitching
Of the victim of a disaster;
The contortions of grief and anguish
In the features of the bereaved.
But we also see
God's Spirit at work,
Bringing new hope into tired despair,
Feeding, comforting, healing,
Giving strength and peace.
And we pray
For a newer, greater concern
For the suffering of the world;
For a search for better priorities
In the use of our resources and love;
For new reasons to smile
And new causes for laughter.

Lord, this is our prayer:
*Help us to know and to do your will.*

With new eyes we look
At ourselves, at the church
And see ourselves clinging
To the pillars of the past,
Afraid of where we will find God
In this fast changing age;
Fearfully hiding behind
Our traditions and worship,
Nervous of that new life
That is the life of faith in Christ,
Lived in union with one another.
But we also see
God's Spirit at work,
Constantly surprising us
With the beauty of old truths

## Fifth Sunday after Epiphany

Revealed in new-born ways.
And we pray
That through us, God's church,
Breathed into life by his Spirit,
Others may hear the Gospel Word
As disturbing, fresh and new,
That together we may walk in hope
Towards the unseen paths of tomorrow.

Lord, this is our prayer:
*Help us to know and to do your will.*

In the name of Jesus Christ our Lord, *Amen.*

# Fifth Sunday after Epiphany

## 2. Work

L: Lord, you have work for each one of us:
R: *Teach us to serve you in all we do.*

Let us pray for those whose daily work gives them power over
other people:
    For those concerned in government;
    For those in charge of companies;
    For the leaders of trades unions;
    For those whose work influences how we think;
    For . . .
Lord, we pray that they may not shirk those responsibilities that go
with their power, and may serve not only their own interests but
those of others, with wisdom, honesty, fairness and kindness.

Lord, you have work for each one of us:
*Teach us to serve you in all we do.*

Let us pray for those who work for the public services in our
society:
    For those who look after our health;
    For those who look after our safety:
    For those who teach and train;
    For those who give us advice and support;
    For those who provide the essentials for life;
    For . . .
Lord, we pray that these people may find satisfaction and joy in
their work, and may serve those they seek to help with patience,
courage and understanding.

Lord, you have work for each one of us:
*Teach us to serve you in all we do.*

Let us pray for those whose work is not rewarded by a wage:
>    For voluntary workers in areas of need;
>    For housewives and parents;
>    For those who raise funds for charities;
>    For those who serve as community leaders;
>    For . . .

Lord, we pray that society may value these people and give them the support that they need. We pray that they may fulfil their duties with humility and generosity of spirit.

Lord, you have work for each one of us:
*Teach us to serve you in all we do.*

Let us pray for those who are finding their work difficult:
>    For those whose jobs are repetitive and dull;
>    For those who cannot get along with their fellow workers;
>    For those who have been put in a moral dilemma;
>    For those who cannot cope with the demands of their work;
>    For . . .

Lord, we pray for those who dread the working day and we ask that you will grant them the courage they need, whether to persevere as they are, or to change their lives.

Lord, you have work for each one of us:
*Teach us to serve you in all we do.*

Lord, we thank you for the lives of those who have died in the Christian faith (for . . . ) and we ask that we may follow their example of faithfulness in the work that we do for your kingdom. Let us pray for those who have been called to work for the church:
>    For ministers and preachers and teachers in every
>       denomination;
>    For all those with responsibility in this church and in the
>       churches of this neighbourhood;
>    For those engaged in mission activity – preaching or educating
>       or healing – at home or abroad;
>    For those who work for Christian organizations and charities:
>    For . . .

Lord, we pray for these people that they may be rich in the faith and hope and love that come from being close to you.

Lord, you have work for each one of us:
*Teach us to serve you in all we do.*

Let us pray for those who are unable to go about their daily lives and work:

> For those who are unemployed;
> For those who are ill ... ;
> For those who have been injured ... ;
> For those recently bereaved ... ;
> For ...

Lord, we pray for these people, whose normal activity has come to a standstill. We ask that you will be with them through the changes in their lives, bringing healing, comfort, hope and meaning.

Lord, you have work for each one of us:
*Teach us to serve you in all we do.*

> Old and young,
> Sick and well,
> Waged and unwaged,
> Academic and labourer,
> Strong and weak:

Lord, you have work for each one of us:
*Teach us to serve you in all we do.*

In the name of Jesus Christ, carpenter, teacher, healer, preacher, our Saviour and your Son, *Amen.*

# Sixth Sunday after Epiphany

## 1. The Right Use of the Sabbath

Lord, there is always so much for us to do.
Time flies past as we rush around.
We never find the time we really need
To relax, to let go, to rest in you.
We are so busy that we feel indispensable
And life overwhelms us, dulls our joy;
We become tired, irritable and tense,
Lash out at others and make mistakes.
Politicians, businessmen, workers,
Housewives, parents, teachers,
Rich and poor, young and old,
We look for rest,
For a time of healing,
For the sabbath time made for us.

*Silence*

Lord, there is always so much for us to do.
Our minds are a-whirl as we rush around.
We never have the time we really need
To stop and think about what we do,
To ask ourselves about our own lives.
We forget the needs of others in your world;
Our consciences blunted by endless action,
We blunder and bluster through life.
Voluntary workers, farmers and shop-keepers,
Sports enthusiasts, avid readers,
Upper, middle and working classes,
We look for opportunities to sit and think,
For time to re-assess our lives,
For the sabbath time made for us.

*Silence*

Lord, there is always so much for us to do.
The world is full of bustle and noise.
We never have the time we really need
To stop and listen to others and to you.
We do not hear the cries of need
Made by our own children in our own homes;
The cries of those suffering elsewhere in the world
Die on the wind.
We cannot share our burdens with others
Because we are unwilling to shoulder theirs.
Academics and manual labourers,
Assembly line workers and skilled craftsmen,
Confident, nervous, mature or adolescent,
We all need to be listened to,
We need time to listen,
The sabbath time made for us.

*Silence*

Lord, there is always so much for us to do
And, running our own lives to our own satisfaction,
We do not have the time we really need
To put you at the centre of our lives.
We push our faith into the background,
Where it is safer, unobtrusive, reassuring.
We are too busy to change our routines
To find room for you and your demands;
It is hard to find the time even to pray.
Powerful and oppressed, sick and well,
Minister and banker and cleaner,
Men and women, black and white,
You long for us,
You are there for us when we call,
When we find sabbath time for you.

*Silence*

In the name of the Lord of the Sabbath, Jesus Christ, *Amen.*

# Sixth Sunday after Epiphany

## 2. *The Holy Mountain*

L: Lord, in your mercy:
R: *Hear our prayer.*

Heavenly Father, we pray
For the shaking up of the power structures of our world,
So that the rules of your kingdom,
Justice, wisdom, mercy and compassion,
May be seen left standing
Amidst the ruins of a fallen confidence
In oppression, force of arms and might.

We pray for . . .

Lord, in your mercy:
*Hear our prayer.*

Heavenly Father, we pray
For the shaking up of the peoples of our world,
So that the vision of your kingdom
Of love and peace, joy and health,
May fill and motivate their lives,
Despite hunger, greed, sickness and war.

We pray for . . .

Lord, in your mercy:
*Hear our prayer.*

Heavenly Father, we pray
For the shaking up of your people, the church.
May the Holy Spirit blow through it
Breathing fresh life into worship,
Revealing those age old truths

That never change or fail us,
Despite the despair and cynicism
Of the shifting times in which we live.

We pray for . . .

Lord, in your mercy:
*Hear our prayer*.

Heavenly Father, we pray
That you might shake up each of us,
Destroying complacency, empty routine,
And help us to re-centre our lives
Around those values and truths that last,
Around a steadfast faith in you;
So that whenever suffering and trouble come
And the storms of life buffet against us
We may be left standing, in you.

Lord, in your mercy:
*Hear our prayer*.

In the name of the Rock of our Salvation, our Lord and Saviour
Jesus Christ, *Amen*.

# Ninth Sunday before Easter
*(Education Sunday)*

## *Christ the Teacher*

L: Lord Jesus, living Parable of God
R: *Make us parables of God for the world.*

Let us pray:
>      for all who teach,
>      at school, college or university,
>      through the written word,
>      through the television or radio:
>      for Sunday School teachers;
>      for preachers;
>      for parents as they bring up their children.

Lord, we pray:
>      that they may educate
>      grown-ups and children
>      to become better citizens of your world,
>      to recognize injustice,
>      oppression and tyranny,
>      to seek government by those who serve the interests of all.

Lord Jesus, living Parable of God:
*Make us parables of God for the world.*

Let us pray:
>      for all who teach,
>      that they may educate
>      grown-ups and children
>      to become responsible members of the family of humankind,
>      to relieve suffering
>      by feeding the hungry,
>      healing the sick,
>      and working together for peace.

Let us pray:
    for all who teach,
    that they may educate
    grown-ups and children
    to find that true knowledge
    which gives reason and purpose to life;
    to find happiness and fulfilment
    in loving and being loved;
    to be open-minded to revelations that could lead to God.

Lord Jesus, living Parable of God:
*Make us parables of God to the world.*

Let us pray:
    for all who teach,
    that they might do so
    with wisdom and patience,
    with honesty and humility;
    never afraid to learn from their own mistakes;
    never afraid to learn from other people;
    faithful to their calling
    to bring truth and understanding.

In the name of Jesus Christ, our Teacher and Example, *Amen*.

# Eighth Sunday before Easter

## *Christit the Healer*

L: Lord, in your mercy:
R: *Hear our prayer.*

As the sick, the disabled, the outcast leper and the mentally disturbed were brought to Christ for healing, so we bring before the Lord in prayer the disease and suffering of our world, and ask for his healing and salvation.

> We pray for diseased countries:
> > ruled with injustice;
> > cowed by fear;
> > chained by oppression.
> For . . .

Lord, in your mercy:
*Hear our prayer.*

> We pray for sick societies:
> > where possessions are put first;
> > where children are abused;
> > where violence stalks the streets.
> For . . .

Lord, in your mercy:
*Hear our prayer.*

> We pray for suffering people:
> > the malnourished and starving;
> > the victims of warfare;
> > the victims of natural disaster.
> For . . .

Lord, in your mercy:
*Hear our prayer.*

We pray for those who are ill:
>   people we know well;
>   people we know only by name;
>   members of this congregation.
For . . .

Lord, in your mercy:
*Hear our prayer.*

We pray for the disabled:
>   seeking fulfilment;
>   seeking understanding;
>   seeking dignity and self-worth.
For . . .

Lord, in your mercy:
*Hear our prayer.*

We pray for those distressed in mind:
>   the bereaved;
>   the depressed and anxious;
>   the hurt and afraid.
For . . .

Lord, in your mercy:
*Hear our prayer.*

We pray for those who seek salvation:
>   those longing for forgiveness;
>   those longing for meaning and a sense of purpose;
>   those longing to know God.
For . . .

Lord, in your mercy:
*Hear our prayer.*

We pray for all those who work to bring healing and wholeness into the lives of nations, of communities, of families and of individuals. We pray for those who bear Christian witness to the salvation to be found through Christ Jesus, as they spread the gospel in word and action, through teaching and preaching, through loving and through healing the sad and the sick.

Lord, in your mercy:
*Hear our prayer.*

## Eighth Sunday before Easter

Loving heavenly Father, through your Son Jesus Christ you met
the needs of those who called upon you with an out-flowing of your
health-giving love. In his name we put into your caring hands the
sickness and the suffering of the world. *Amen.*

# Seventh Sunday before Easter

## Christ, Worker of Miracles

Lord, you constantly surprise us,
Answering our prayers in ways
We had not asked or thought;
Changing people and their lives
Beyond all our expectations.
We gasp at the joy we find in you
In the face of evil and suffering,
We marvel at your miraculous love
    bringing hope out of despair;
    bringing health out of sickness;
    bringing life out of death.

We need your miracles, Lord,
In a world stale with bad news.
We need the miracles
Of the hidden power of your love,
Working secretly, slowly, unseen,
In the hearts of humankind,
Attracting governments and leaders
To a vision of the future
Where the nations will be ruled
With justice, wisdom and care;
Working secretly, slowly, unseen,
Opening our eyes to see
The plight of the hungry,
Opening our ears to hear
The cries of the distressed,
Opening our hands to give
Where help is needed,
Opening our hearts to love
As you first loved us;
Working secretly, slowly, unseen,

*Seventh Sunday before Easter*

Your Spirit within our churches,
Disturbing us, changing us,
Turning us outward,
Pushing and pulling us on:
We need the miracle
Of the hidden power of your love
Working secretly, slowly, unseen.

We need your miracles, Lord,
In a world stale with bad news.
We need miracles of your love
That shock and shake us up,
Coming suddenly, strangely, in full view:
The coming of a startling event
That changes the ways of a nation;
The coming of one person
That starts a freedom movement;
The coming of a cry for help
That leads to tremendous giving;
The coming of life and health
To the sick and depressed;
The coming of forgiveness
In a situation of hatred;
The coming of God's Spirit afresh,
Into dreary, exhausted lives.
We need the miracles of your love
That shock and shake us up,
Coming suddenly, strangely, in full view.

Surprise us again, Lord,
Work your miracles in us,
Work your miracles through us.

In the name of our Saviour, Jesus Christ, *Amen.*

# Ash Wednesday

L: Lord, hear us:
*R: Lord, graciously hear us.*

Lord, we were blind
And still we do not see
As we should:
We long to close our eyes
To the injustice all around us;
To the politics of might
That victimize the powerless;
To the greed of societies
Who grind the face of the poor.

Lord, we pray
That you may open the eyes
Of the peoples of the world
And their leaders,
That we may see what is right
And act for the good.

Lord, hear us:
*Lord, graciously hear us.*

Lord, we were deaf
And still we do not hear
As we should:
We shut out
The cries of the needy
Where the voice of Christ
Is to be found.

Lord, we pray
That you may open our ears
To the clamouring of the hungry,

## Ash Wednesday

To the complaints
Of those we neglect,
To the sobbing
Of the desperately unhappy,
To your call to minister
To those for whom Christ died.

Lord, hear us:
*Lord, graciously hear us.*

Lord, we were heavily burdened
And still we carry much
Because we lack in faith.
We bring to you
Our burdens of anxiety
And lay them at your feet;
We bring to you
The people for whom we care
Who are ill, sad or afraid;
We pray for . . .

Lord, we pray
That you will lift all our burdens
And increase our faith
That, travelling light,
We may always be ready
To go where you call.

Lord, hear us:
*Lord, graciously hear us.*

In Jesus' name, *Amen.*

# Sixth Sunday before Easter
*(Lent 1)*

## The King and the Kingdom: Temptation

L: You, Lord, are our strength and vision:
*R: Lead us out of temptation.*

The temptation
To abuse the power of leadership:
Ruling by force
Instead of consent;
Calling injustice
An expedient tactic;
Treating human subjects
As mere objects;
Preaching nationalism
Not co-operation
Or peace.

You, Lord, are our strength and vision:
*Lead us out of temptation.*

The temptation
To turn a deaf ear and a blind eye
To the cries of the tortured;
To the matchstick arms and legs
Of a starving child;
To warnings of future disaster;
To the lonely face
At the window next door;
To the challenge
Of the sounds and sights
Of our suffering world.

You, Lord, are our strength and vision:
*Lead us out of temptation.*

The temptation
To betray the calling of the church:
Refusing to meet
People's real needs;
Looking inwards and backwards
But not outwards and forwards;
Becoming exclusive
Instead of all-embracing;
Being afraid to share
The Life and the words
Of faith.

You, Lord, are our strength and vision:
*Lead us out of temptation.*

The temptation
To sheer away from
The troubled questioning
    of the sick
    of the bereaved
    of the anxious
    of the depressed
    of the dying
    of those who have lost
    their faith in you.

You, Lord, are our strength and vision:
*Lead us out of temptation.*

The temptation
To refuse the offer
Of real life in you;
To remain less
Than you call us to be;
To walk with narrowed vision
Along a path of fear;
To love sparingly;
To be wary of others;
To be wary of you.

You, Lord, are our strength and vision:
*Lead us out of temptation.*

Lord, we are all surrounded by temptations of many kinds,
temptations that would lead us to do harm to ourselves or others,

or to neglect to do what is good. We pray that we may learn how to use aright our power to choose what we do and say. We make our prayer in the name of Jesus Christ, who was tempted to exploit the power of God within him, but resisted and followed the servant path to death and lives and reigns our Risen Lord and Saviour. *Amen.*

# Fifth Sunday before Easter
## *(Lent 2)*

### *The King and the Kingdom: Conflict*

Lord,
We know that you want us
To pray for our world
Torn apart by conflict,
To pray for peace,
For harmony,
For love;

But we can't even agree
On exactly what
We should be praying for . . .
And some of us
Are angry with you
That things are
As they are.

There is conflict
Within your church:
All major systems
Of organization, of doctrine,
Have their noisy dissidents;
All forms of Christian action
Have righteous supporters
And righteous opponents;
And we don't always
Like one another much,
Either!

Lord, where are you?
Is it you on this side
Or are you on that?
Or are you in the middle
Of the conflict,

Being torn apart
By the hands that reach out
For your hands
But pull away
From one another?

Lord, we pray for the church.

(*Silence*)

There is conflict
Within the world:
Nations spend
Their life's blood
On weapons to defend themselves
Against one another.
There is conflict
Within nations,
Within communities and
Within families,
Conflicts of hatred,
Conflicts of love.

Lord, where are you?
Is it you on this side
Or are you on that?
There are no sides
To the Cross,
Just arms outstretched.
There you hang,
Crucified by those who loved you,
And knew they had done wrong
In denying you;
Crucified by those who hated you
And knew they were right
In having you killed.

Lord, we pray for the world.

(*Silence*)

There is conflict
In our own lives;
The call to be responsible
Eats into our peace:
How should we spend our money,

## Fifth Sunday before Easter

Spend our time,
When the myriad begging bowls
Of the world
Are piled around our feet?
Within us
There is constant warfare
But we cannot always tell
Which side is yours.

Lord, where are you?
Is it you on this side
Or are you on that?
We see you on both,
The Prince of Peace
Wielding a sword!
Life with you is not peaceful,
But our only real peace
Is to be found in you,
Within real life.

Lord, we pray for ourselves.

(*Silence*)

Lord, we pray for all those whose lives are in conflict – who fight against others, against injustice, against those they love, against hunger, against their own fears, against illness. We ask that they may be aware of your love, from which nothing can ever separate us. In the name of Jesus, *Amen*.

# Fourth Sunday before Easter
*(Lent 3)*

## The King and the Kingdom: Suffering

L: Lord, in your mercy:
R: *Hear our prayer.*

Let us pray
for those who suffer
at the hands of others:
those who live
under unjust regimes,
who are persecuted, beaten,
tortured and imprisoned
for being what they are
or believing what they believe.
(For . . . )

In the name of Christ,
the scourged, the mocked, the crucified,
Lord, in your mercy:
*Hear our prayer.*

Let us pray
for those who suffer
as the victims of warfare:
those who are physically
or psychologically scarred,
children taught to hate
and adults to live in death's shadow.
We pray for the widowed,
the orphaned,
for homeless refugees.
(For . . . )

## Fourth Sunday before Easter

In the name of Christ,
who wept over the city of Jerusalem
because she was to fall,
Lord, in your mercy:
*Hear our prayer.*

Let us pray
for those who suffer
from the harshness of nature:
those who are born disabled,
those who are the victims
of earthquake or flood,
of drought or famine.
We pray for those who are ill
and for those who are dying.
(For . . . )

In the name of Christ,
who healed those brought to him,
Lord, in your mercy:
*Hear our prayer*

Let us pray
for those who suffer
through the selfishness
of others:
those who starve
while others eat too well,
those who are lonely
while others are too busy to care,
those who are neglected
because their voice is small.
(For . . . )

In the name of Christ,
who lived for others,
Lord, in your mercy:
*Hear our prayer.*

Let us pray
for those who suffer
because they love:
for the bereaved
and those who are anxious

76

about relatives or friends,
for those who weep
at the evils of the world,
for those who deny themselves
to give loving care.
(For . . . )

In the name of Christ,
who gave himself on the Cross
in obedience to love,
Lord, in your mercy:
*Hear our prayer.*

Let us pray
for those who suffer
because of their own actions:
those who suffer guilt,
whose lives are full of regret,
those who despise
the people they are,
those who have made themselves
unloving or unloveable.
(For . . . )

In the name of Christ,
who pronounced the forgiveness of sins,
Lord, in your mercy:
*Hear our prayer.*

Lord, we rejoice that through the ages your saints have been
prepared to suffer as they followed your way of love. We pray that
we, encouraged by their faithful witness, may be ready to give all
in the service of your eternal kingdom of love.

In the name of Christ,
who called for his disciples
to take up the Cross,
Lord, in your mercy:
*Hear our prayer.*

Lord, on the Cross of Christ we see you sharing in the suffering of
your world. We rejoice to know that in our darkest hours you are
with us, and we commend into your love those whom we know
who are suffering in any way. *Amen.*

# Third Sunday before Easter
*(Lent 4)*

## *The King and the Kingdom: Transfiguration*

L: Lord, reveal your glory to the world:
R: *The glory of suffering, healing love.*

> Lord,
> we pray for the nations
> who glory in the display
> of their might:
> the gleaming weapons,
> the polished guns,
> made to shed blood,
> to burn human flesh.

Lord, reveal your glory to the world:
*The glory of suffering, healing love.*

> Lord,
> we pray for the nations
> who glory in the display
> of their wealth:
> the shining edifices
> built for the powerful,
> the shops bejewelled
> with exotic, foreign food,
> while the houses of the poor
> moulder and crumble,
> and the peoples abroad
> hunger and starve.

Lord, reveal your glory to the world:
*The glory of suffering, healing love.*

Lord,
we pray for the church
glorying in the brightness
of fellowship and worship:
the colour and custom
of Christmas and Harvest,
the cheerful noise
of enjoyable praise
sometimes drowning
the voice of challenge,
sometimes covering over
the darkness of sin,
the reality of pain and despair.

Lord, reveal your glory to the world:
*The glory of suffering, healing love.*

Lord,
we pray for our society,
which glories in success,
the spacious home
in the clean, green suburb,
the sparkling ornaments
of travel, clothes and cars,
while those who feel
the strain of keeping up
or the pain of failure
resort to the bottle,
to solvents or drugs,
to give false glory
to grey, troubled lives.

Lord, reveal your glory to the world:
*The glory of suffering, healing love.*

Lord, teach us to glory only in you, that our lives, however dull
and hard they may seem, may be transfigured into the glorious life
of your kingdom. In Christ's name, *Amen.*

# Second Sunday before Easter
*(Passion Sunday)*

### The King and the Kingdom: Victory of the Cross

L: In our struggles with the enemies of humanity
R: *We claim the victory of the Cross*
L: And offer ourselves for God's cause.

> Lord,
> we name before you
> the enemies of humanity
> that deny our human rights:
>
> Injustice;
> (*Silence*)
> Oppression;
> (*Silence*)
> Persecution;
> (*Silence*)
> Exploitation.
> (*Silence*)

In our struggles with the enemies of humanity
*We claim the victory of the Cross*
And offer ourselves for God's cause.

> *Silence*
>
> Lord,
> we name before you
> the enemies of humanity
> that turn life into mere existence:
>
> Hunger;
> (*Silence*)
> Homelessness;
> (*Silence*)

Warfare;
(*Silence*)
Loneliness.
(*Silence*)

In our struggles with the enemies of humanity
*We claim the victory of the cross*
And offer ourselves for God's cause.

*Silence*

Lord,
we name before you
the enemies of humanity
that attack your church:

Divisiveness;
(*Silence*)
Apathy;
(*Silence*)
Hypocrisy;
(*Silence*)
Lack of faith.
(*Silence*)

In our struggles with the enemies of humanity
*We claim the victory of the cross*
And offer ourselves for God's cause.

*Silence*

Lord,
we name before you
the enemies of humanity
that strike us in times of trouble,
of illness, anxiety or loss,
and threaten to overwhelm us:

Despair;
(*Silence*)
Bitterness;
(*Silence*)
Guilt;
(*Silence*)
Cynicism.
(*Silence*)

*Second Sunday before Easter*

In our struggles with the enemies of humanity
*We claim the victory of the cross*
And offer ourselves for God's cause.

> *Silence*

> Lord,
> we name before you
> the enemies of humanity
> that bring misery to the whole world:

> Greed;
> (*Silence*)
> Hatred;
> (*Silence*)
> Fear;
> (*Silence*)
> Ignorance.
> (*Silence*)

In our struggles with the enemies of humanity
*We claim the victory of the cross*
And offer ourselves for God's cause.

> *Silence*

> Lord, in silence
> we name before you
> the enemies of the humanity
> within us.

> *Silence*

In our struggles with the enemies of humanity
*We claim the victory of the cross*
And offer ourselves for God's cause.

> *Silence*

Father, in the offering of your Son, Jesus Christ, upon the cross, you triumphed over the powers of sin and death. Help us so to claim the power of that victory within our lives that the world may know of your kingdom of life and love and peace. *Amen.*

# The Sunday before Easter
## (Palm Sunday)

### The Way of the Cross

The world judges
By its fears and its hopes.

In hope, the world cries hosanna to Christ;
In fear, it condemns him to death.

Let us pray
for those who judge themselves in hope:
who take up their cross on life's uphill journey,
making footholds from victories and failures alike;
who humbly and joyfully press on.
Let us pray
for those who judge themselves in fear:
who find each failure or weakness
a reason for guilt and despair;
who shy away from the uphill climb
for fear of falling;
who dare not lift the heavy cross
for fear they will prove too weak.

Lord, under you we shall do valiantly.

(*Silence*)

In hope, the world cries hosanna to Christ;
In fear, it condemns him to death.

Let us pray
for those who judge their society in hope:
seeing poverty – they strive for justice;
seeing oppression – they campaign for liberty;
seeing blindness – they work to enlighten;
in hope they shoulder the cross
of loving responsibility.

## The Sunday before Easter

Let us pray
for those who judge their society in fear:
clinging to material prosperity – they condone injustice;
clinging to power – they exercise oppression;
clinging to false values and doctrines –
they turn a blind eye to the realities of life;
in fear they crucify
all that brings glimpses of hope.

Lord, under you we shall do valiantly.

(*Silence*)

In hope, the world cries hosanna to Christ;
In fear, it condemns him to death.

Let us pray
for those who judge the church in hope:
who challenge us to take the Way of the Cross
and show Resurrection power in their own lives;
who make us feel uncomfortable
but comfort us in our troubles;
who diagnose our sickness
and lead us to him who heals;
who spend themselves for us.
Let us pray
for those who judge the church in fear:
calling it unfriendly, hypocritical,
idealistic and dull,
when they, too, are afraid of commitment
and of the absolute demands of love;
when cynicism distorts their own vision
robbing the Cross of its glory and strange joy.

Lord, under you we shall do valiantly.

(*Silence*)

In hope the world cries hosanna to Christ;
In fear, it condemns him to death.

Hosanna to our crucified, risen Lord! *Amen.*

# Thursday before Easter
## (Maundy Thursday)

### The Upper Room

L: Wash us, Lord,
    Feed us with your love:
*R: Unite us with Christ,*
    *Give us hope for the world.*

Lord, your disciples are coming to you.
Our feet are dirty from the paths we have trodden.
Our hearts are hungry for you.

Wash us, Lord,
Feed us with your love:
*Unite us with Christ,*
*Give us hope for the world.*

Our feet are dirty
from the paths of everyday life,
from making the wrong compromises
when faced with important decisions,
from not giving time or energy
to those whom we need and love,
from running fast to get away from you
or dawdling in the hope of being left behind!
Our hearts are hungry for you,
for the assurance of knowing we are loved,
for the belief there is a purpose in life.
We need: the peace,
          the strength,
          the joy,
               that come from you.

Wash us, Lord,
Feed us with your love:
*Unite us with Christ,*
*Give us hope for the world.*

## Thursday before Easter

Our feet are dirty
from the paths of suffering;
the experience and knowledge of pain
clings to us and darkens our lives.
Illness, starvation, natural disaster,
bereavement, handicaps, war ...
the stones on life's path
cause us to bleed.
Our hearts are hungry for you,
for the bread and wine we share together,
symbols of the suffering you share with us.
We need: the courage,
        the compassion,
        the faith,
                that come from you.

Wash us, Lord,
Feed us with your love:
*Unite us with Christ,*
*Give us hope for the world.*

Our feet are dirty
from the ways of our world,
from standing idly by:
while injustice and oppression
besmirch so many lands;
while the wealthy exploit the poor
who lie down hungry in the dust to die.
Our hearts are hungry for you,
for the sacrifice of your love
that leads us into your kingdom.
We need: the wisdom,
        the justice,
        the love,
                that come from you.

Wash us, Lord,
Feed us with your love:
*Unite us with Christ,*
*Give us hope for the world.*

In the name of Christ
    the Living Water,
    the Bread of Life,
    the True Vine,
      *Amen.*

# Good Friday

## The Death of Christ

'Father, forgive them for they know not what they do.'

Father,
within our world
your principles of
       love,
       justice,
       mercy
       and compassion
are crucified every day
and in every land
by powerful people
who do not really understand
what they are doing to others,
what they are doing to you.

We pray for all those
who suffer today
as the result
of the actions of others;
the victims of
       greed,
       violence,
       warfare,
       oppression,
       injustice.

*Silence*

'When Jesus saw his mother and the disciple whom he loved
standing near, he said to his mother, "Woman, behold your son!"
Then he said to the disciple, "Behold your mother!"'

Father,
we pray for our family, the church.
United by our love for you
may we be united in love for one another.
We bring before you
our Christian brothers and sisters,
from every land and race,
who are suffering today:
those who are persecuted;
those who are in need;
those engaged in costly service.
We pray for the church here in . . .
and for those from this congregation
who are suffering in any way.

*Silence*

'My God, my God, why have you forsaken me?'

Father,
we pray for those
who know the suffering
of total despair:
for the terminally ill
and the grief-stricken;
for the depressed
and those consumed by guilt;
for those who have lost their faith
in life, in others, in you.
We bring before you
those who feel totally alone
when faced with fears and pain
that threaten to overwhelm them.

*Silence*

'It is finished.'

Father,
we pray
that you will fill each one of us
with the life of your Spirit,
so that we may respond
to the calls that you give
and follow your Son

## Good Friday

on his healing,
    teaching,
    forgiving,
    accepting,
    suffering way of love for others
until the end of our lives,
and on into life everlasting
with you.

*Silence*

In the name of our crucified Saviour, our Risen and Living Lord, Jesus Christ, *Amen.*

# Easter Day

## The Resurrection of Christ

L: Risen Lord, set free in the world:
*R: Roll away the stone from our tomb.*

There is a tomb,
carved from the rock of oppression,
where the dignity of humankind
lies buried.

Risen Lord, set free in the world:
*Roll away the stone from our tomb.*

There is a tomb,
carved from the rock of indifference,
where compassion for those in need
lies buried.

Risen Lord, set free in the world:
*Roll away the stone from our tomb.*

There is a tomb,
carved from the rock of fear,
where the peace of each person and of the world,
lies buried.

Risen Lord, set free in the world:
*Roll away the stone from our tomb.*

There is a tomb,
carved from the rock of suffering,
where the joys of life and loving
lie buried.

Risen Lord, set free in the world:
*Roll away the stone from our tomb.*

## Easter Day

There is a tomb,
carved from the rock of death,
where the creativity and warmth of life
lie buried.

Risen Lord, set free in the world:
*Roll away the stone from our tomb.*

There is a tomb,
carved from the rock of guilt,
where feelings of self-worth and value
lie buried.

Risen Lord, set free in the world:
*Roll away the stone from our tomb.*

We ask, Father, for your resurrection life for the world – that love
and life and joy and peace may triumph over sin and death.

In the name of Christ the Victorious, *Amen.*

# Easter Day

## *The Resurrection of Christ*

L: The Lord hears our prayer:
*R: Thanks be to God.*

On this Easter Day,
let us pray
for life for the world,
life triumphant over:
>>> persecution
>>> illness
>>> suffering
>>> death

*Silence*

The Lord hears our prayer:
*Thanks be to God.*

On this Easter Day,
let us pray
for love for the world,
love triumphant over:
>>> indifference
>>> selfishness
>>> hatred
>>> death

*Silence*

The Lord hears our prayer:
*Thanks be to God.*

On this Easter Day,
let us pray
for peace for the world,

peace triumphant over:
> fear
> warfare
> inner conflict
> death

*Silence*

The Lord hears our prayer:
*Thanks be to God.*

On this Easter Day,
let us pray
for joy for the world,
joy triumphant over:
> despair
> frustration
> deprivation
> death

*Silence*

The Lord hears our prayer:
*Thanks be to God.*

On this Easter Day,
let us pray
for salvation for the world,
salvation triumphant over:
> sin
> pollution
> disease
> death

*Silence*

The Lord hears our prayer:
*Thanks be to God.*

We make our prayers in the name of our risen Lord and Saviour,
Jesus Christ. *Amen.*

# The Sunday after Easter

## 1. The Upper Room Appearances

L: Crucified and risen Lord, reveal yourself to us:
*R: That we may be faithful and believing.*

Lord, we are riddled with doubts
About you and your trustworthiness,
Your goodness, your power, your existence.
Sometimes what we see, feel and learn
Affirms your living, loving presence;
Sometimes the reality of evil and suffering
And the shallowness of our daily lives
Make us doubt, or leave us afraid.

Crucified and risen Lord, reveal yourself to us:
*That we may be faithful and believing.*

Lord, we are riddled with doubts
About ourselves and our lives.
We feel that we have lost control
Over our future, over what we are.
Ruled by emotions, by fear or apathy,
Governed by circumstances, responsibilities,
Frustrated by illness, or lack of ability,
We are not what we wish we were,
We do not know whether, or how, to change.

Crucified and risen Lord, reveal yourself to us:
*That we may be faithful and believing.*

Lord, we are riddled with doubts
About your body, the church;
About our future in an age
Which rejects our beliefs and values;
About our mission, in a troubled world

Where so many need help and support,
But where the issues are complicated
And we feel powerless and small.

Crucified and risen Lord, reveal yourself to us:
*That we might be faithful and believing.*

Lord, we are riddled with doubts
About the fate of humankind:
We see hunger caused by others' greed;
We see the ravages of diseases
Made worse by the ways we choose to live;
We see growing evidence of violence
Within communities once tight-knit;
We see addiction to drugs and alcohol
And indifference to people's real needs.

Crucified and risen Lord, reveal yourself to us:
*That we might be faithful and believing.*

Lord, we are riddled with doubts
About the future of our world:
A world polluted and plundered
Over successive generations;
A world faced with total destruction
At the unleashing of nuclear war;
A world where economic forces
Rule the hearts and minds of nations;
A world where nation strives against nation
And no one knows who is friend or foe.

Crucified and risen Lord, reveal yourself to us:
*That we might be faithful and believing.*

Heavenly Father, we know that you have not promised us an easy
life, but you have promised that, whatever happens, nothing can
separate us from your love. We ask that you will keep us alive in
this faith. In the name of your faithful Son, Jesus Christ our Lord
and Saviour. *Amen.*

# The Sunday after Easter

## 2. *The Bread of Life*

L: Lord, in your mercy:
*R: Hear our prayer.*

Let us pray
for the hungry in our world,
that they may be satisfied.

Lord, we pray
for those who hunger for justice:
the black child deprived of opportunities;
the poet denied freedom of expression;
the farmer whose lands have been taken away;
the believer forced to hide the faith;
the poor whose work brings little reward.

We pray for . . .

Father, feed us with the Bread of Life
that we may hunger no more.

Lord, in your mercy:
*Hear our prayer.*

Lord, we pray
for those who hunger for the necessities of life:
the starving child in a drought-ridden land;
the homeless refugee fleeing from war;
the old man who cannot pay to heat his home;
the anorexic teenager, unable to eat;
the vagrant who buys alcohol instead of food.

We pray for . . .

Father, feed us with the Bread of Life
that we may hunger no more.

Lord, in your mercy:
*Hear our prayer.*

Lord, we pray
for those who hunger for healing:
for the child in pain or discomfort;
for the mother in the depths of depression;
for the frightened boy rushed into hospital;
for the injured coming to terms with disability;
for the dying man longing for a good death.

We pray for . . .

Father, feed us with the Bread of Life
that we may hunger no more.

Lord, in your mercy:
*Hear our prayer.*

Lord, we pray
for those who hunger for peace:
for the child whose parents constantly argue;
for the woman campaigning for world peace;
for the man in a stressful occupation;
for the sleepless sufferer of anxiety;
for the hectic worker with no time to rest.

We pray for . . .

Father, feed us with the Bread of Life
that we may hunger no more.

Lord, in your mercy:
*Hear our prayer.*

Lord, we pray
for those who hunger for love:
the child abused and neglected by parents;
the stranger whom no one befriends;
the elderly who have lost life-companions;
the lonely, isolated by fear or shyness;
each one of us, needing someone else.

We pray for . . .

Father, feed us with the Bread of Life
that we may hunger no more.

Lord, in your mercy:
*Hear our prayer.*

Lord, we pray
for those who hunger for you:
the child praying out of helplessness;
the young man with no sense of purpose;
the woman earnestly seeking faith;
the bereaved who feel you have withdrawn;
the tired old man, waiting to greet death.

We pray for . . .

Father, feed us with the Bread of Life
that we may hunger no more.

Lord, in your mercy:
*Hear our prayer.*

Father, only feed us with the Bread of Life, your Son and our
Saviour Jesus Christ, and we shall be satisfied. We ask it in his
name. *Amen.*

# Second Sunday after Easter

## 1. The Emmaus Road

L: Lord, this is our prayer:
*Help us to know and to do your will.*

We talk together, Lord
About the recent news,
The good news, the bad news
That invades our homes,
Bursting forth from radio
Or from television.

We pray
About those events in the world
That are in our news today . . .

Join in our conversations, Lord,
Make your presence known in the world.

Lord, this is our prayer:
*Help us to know and to do your will.*

We talk together, Lord,
About people we know,
Sharing in their joys,
Sharing in their sorrows.
We hear of illness,
Of anxiety, of death.

We pray
for those whom we know
who are suffering in any way
for . . .

Join in our conversations, Lord,
Make your presence known in the world.

Lord, this is our prayer:
*Help us to know and to do your will.*

We talk together, Lord,
About our faith in you;
In our Sunday services,
In our fellowship meetings,
With friends in our homes.
We seek you together.

We pray
for the worship in our church
for the spreading of your good news
for . . .

Join in our conversations, Lord,
Make your presence known in the world.

Lord, this is our prayer:
*Help us to know and to do your will.*

Lord, you talk to us,
Walk with us,
Break bread with us
And constantly surprise us
With the eternal power
Of your resurrection,
Which brings good news from bad,
Health from sickness,
Life from death,
Joy from sorrow.
We pray for a world
Full of despair and violence,
For the human race
Who suffer and sorrow,
For a church prone
to apathy and fear.

Join in our conversations, Lord,
Make your presence known in the world.

Lord, this is our prayer:
*Help us to know and to do your will.*

In the name of him who travels with us along every road, our
Risen Lord, Jesus Christ, *Amen.*

# Second Sunday after Easter

## 2. *The Good Shepherd*

Lord, we ask
For the courage of the Good Shepherd,
Who lays down his life for his sheep.
We pray for those prepared to suffer
And even to die
For what they believe in.
(For . . . )
*Silence*
We pray for those whose lives
And rights are sacrificed
In the name of power and greed.
(For . . . )
*Silence*
We pray for those who risk themselves
By accompanying others
Along paths of deep suffering,
Through valleys of fear and despair.
(For . . . )
*Silence*

Lord, we ask
For the compassion of the Good Shepherd,
Who leads his sheep to safe pasture.
We pray for those who work
To feed and shelter and educate
The poor peoples of our world.
(For . . . )
*Silence*
We pray for those skilled
At nursing and healing
Those who are suffering or ill

In body, mind or spirit.
(For . . . )
*Silence*
We pray for those who care
For the victims of our society,
Those unable to cope with life,
The neglected, the abused.
(For . . . )
*Silence*

Lord, we ask
For the love of the Good Shepherd
Who knows his sheep by name.
We pray for our church,
For its minister and stewards,
For its preachers and teachers,
And all engaged in pastoral care.
(For . . . )
*Silence*
We pray for those we know,
Relatives or friends,
Who are facing difficult times.
(For . . . )
*Silence*
We pray for ourselves
That we might hear the call
From our Good Shepherd
And follow his way of love.
*Silence.*

We make all our prayers in Christ's name. *Amen.*

# Third Sunday after Easter

## 1. The Lakeside

> L: Lord, in our daily lives and work
> R: *Be with us, call us, guide us.*

'When the alarm goes off, I feel my heart sink. I feel leaden inside
at the prospect of getting up and facing another day at work. It
feels as if I am sacrificing all the joy in my life – yet I need to go out
and earn for my family, for my own self-respect.'

> Lord, we pray for those
> whose work seems
> dull and unproductive;
> for those tied to jobs
> they find depressing
> by their need to earn;
> for those frustrated
> by working in positions
> that do not stretch them
> or use their potential;
> for those who struggle
> to cope with the stress
> their jobs entail.

Lord, in our daily lives and work
*Be with us, call us, guide us.*

'I find it hard, being a Christian, in my line of work. The decisions
I have to make are not based on love or kindness. I am not even
sure that my business serves the community in any meaningful
way. And am I entitled to earn all the money I do?'

> Lord, we pray for those
> whose daily work
> puts them in moral dilemmas:

for those ordered to do
what they think to be
morally suspect or wrong;
for those responsible
for hiring and firing
in a society where
employment is scarce;
for those forced to compromise
with their consciences
through economic necessity;
for those who cannot believe
in what they are doing.

Lord, in our daily lives and work:
*Be with us, call us, guide us.*

'I have tried to find work, but offering myself only to be rejected
has left me feeling hurt and useless. I am a burden, to the state, my
family and myself. What am I going to do, with no money and no
future?'

Lord, we pray for those
who are unemployed:
for the young
who have little chance
of starting their chosen career;
for those with families
where the lack of money
causes intolerable strain;
for the middle-aged
who are labelled 'old',
who find that their
experience is unwanted;
for all those who feel
less of a person,
having no job
to give them a name.

Lord, in our daily lives and work:
*Be with us, call us, guide us.*

'I am too busy to sit and talk, too busy to read and think, too busy to enjoy the simple things of life. You often cannot reach me because the line is engaged. I have lots of acquaintances, but few friends. I know what I do – but I'm not sure what I am.'

> Lord, we pray for those
> who are always busy,
> who work to find purpose,
> but risk losing themselves:
> for those whose work restricts
> the depth of their relationships
> with family and friends;
> for those unable
> to rest and relax
> or to find inner peace
> in everyday life;
> for those whose consciences
> see justification only
> in never-ending labour;
> for those who live
> only to work.

> Lord, in our daily lives and work:
> *Be with us, call us, guide us.*

'After that glorious Easter-time – what were we to do next? The practicalities of daily life could not be ignored – so back to work we went. Yet without him our work proved fruitless. Only when he called and guided us did our new life's work begin.'

Lord, we seek you not only on Sundays, but on every day and in every place. We seek you in our church life and service, in our homes, our work and our leisure.

> Lord, in our daily lives and work:
> *Be with us, call us, guide us.*

In the name of Jesus Christ, *Amen.*

# Third Sunday after Easter

## 2. The Resurrection and the Life

L: Lord, in your mercy:
*R: Hear our prayer.*

Lord, we pray for those who are dying:
Those on the threshold of death's door,
And those who have learnt they are to die.
We pray for those with terminal illness,
For those who are badly injured,
For those struck down in a moment.

Lord, we pray
That these people may experience
The life to be found in you,
A life stronger than death itself.
We pray
That last days may be lived
In dignity and peace;
That the dying may be given
Resources of hope and courage;
That they may be surrounded
By those who love and care,
By those ready to listen
And to reassure.

Lord, in your mercy:
*Hear our prayer.*

Lord, we pray for those who are bereaved:
Those who have just lost someone they love
And those who still ache after many long days. months
We pray for those who had expected death to come
And those shocked by unexpected loss;
Those who have lost a life's companion;
Those who have lost a young child.

Lord, we pray
That these people may experience
The life to be found in you,
A life stronger than death itself.
We pray
That they may receive comfort and support
From those who care and understand;
That they may be able to express their grief
And so begin to find healing and hope;
That they may find God's love
In their pain and deepest sorrow,
Driving away hatred and bitterness,
Lifting guilt and anger and regret.

Lord, in your mercy:
*Hear our prayer.*

Lord, we pray for those who are prepared to die
For the causes in which they believe
Or for the people they feel called to serve.
We pray for those opposing oppressive governments;
For those who risk all to rescue others;
For believers persecuted for their faith.

Lord, we pray
That these people may experience
The life to be found in you,
A life stronger than death itself.
We pray
That their vision and courage
May bring truth and justice;
That there may be freedom
For persecuted humankind:
That life may be seen
As a sacred gift
To be used well
In the service of love.

Lord, in your mercy:
*Hear our prayer.*

Lord, we pray for those who long for death,
Who find their lives unbearable
And feel they would prefer to die:
Those who are deeply depressed;

108

Those in overwhelming pain;
Those suffering bereavement and loss;
Those racked with guilt or fear.

— Those who have lost meaning.

Lord, we pray
That these people may experience
The life to be found in you,
A life stronger than death itself.
We pray
For healing for the depressed;
For release for those in pain;
For the dawning of new hope
To those who are bereaved;
For the knowledge of forgiveness
For those tortured with guilt;
And the comfort of God's presence
For those who are afraid.

Lord, in your mercy:
*Hear our prayer.*

We make our prayers with the whole community of the faithful
and with those who have departed this earthly life; praying in the
name of him who leads us on to God's eternal kingdom, who is the
Resurrection and the Life, our Lord and Saviour, Jesus Christ.
*Amen.*

# Fourth Sunday after Easter

## 1. The Charge to Peter

L: Lord, we love you:
R: *Help us to care for your world.*

Lord, we pray
for those who are charged
to care for the welfare of nations:
for the United Nations' Organization;
for governments and leaders;
for all who vote at elections.
We pray that, working together,
they may bring an age of peace, ~~about~~
when each person and each society
feels secure in a world
where justice, wisdom and compassion reign.

Lord, we love you:
*Help us to care for your world.*

Lord, we pray
for those who are charged
to care for the needy:
for those who feed and minister to
the hungry in other lands;
for those who help and counsel
the poor and those unable to cope;
for all those who raise money
to pay for caring work.
We pray that in our search
for a fairer sharing of the earth's wealth
we may be granted the vision
of an age without hunger and want.

give us Lord a
desire to inconvenience
ourselves to bring some
support + others.

110

Lord, we love you:
*Help us to care for your world.*

Lord, we pray
for those who are charged
to care for the sick and the dying,
the confused and the disabled:
for those who nurse relatives at home;
for the staff, doctors and nurses
in hospitals, homes and hospices;
for hospital chaplains and visitors.
We pray that as we give
comfort and hope to those who are ill
we may learn that health and wholeness,
our complete salvation, is to be found
in our Risen Lord, Jesus Christ.

Lord, we love you:
*Help us to care for your world.*

Lord, we pray
for those who are charged
to care for children:
for parents and guardians;
for those who work in children's homes;
for Sunday School teachers and youth leaders;
for social workers and probation officers;
for all those who work to provide education.
We pray that, as we together
take responsibility for the nation's children,
we may begin to build a society
where each child is nurtured and loved.

Lord, we love you:
*Help us to care for your world.*

Lord, we pray    + teach, encourage + challenge
for those who are charged
to care for the church:
for ministers and leaders;
for stewards and teachers;
for all those engaged in pastoral work,    may they care, may they feed
visiting the sick, being with the bereaved,    may they build up each
listening to the troubled, anxious and depressed.    other up in love
We pray that in our service together    may they point the
way to Christ.

111

### Fourth Sunday after Easter

we may be obedient disciples of Christ,
fulfilling his charge to Peter
by tending and feeding his sheep.

Lord, we love you:
*Help us to care for your world.*

In the name of our Good Shepherd, Jesus Christ, *Amen.*

112

# Fourth Sunday after Easter

## 2. *The Way, the Truth and the Life*

L: Lord, this is our prayer:
R: *Help us to know and to do your will.*

> You, Lord, are the Way
> And though you are no easy way
> We pray that the world
> Might follow your path:
> The path of suffering
> That leads to salvation;
> The path of sorrow
> That leads to joy;
> The path of death
> That leads to life;
> The path of self-giving
> That leads to true gain.

We pray for all those in our world who undergo suffering and are prepared to die opposing the injustice, oppression and greed of others.

We pray for all those who sorrow at the evil in the world and for the misfortunes of others. We pray for those who sorrow alongside the suffering and the bereaved.

We pray for all those who give themselves in order to serve and care for and love those in need.

We pray that we, too, may have the courage to walk on Christ's Way.

Lord, this is our prayer:
*Help us to know and to do your will.*

113

> You, Lord, are the Truth
> And although your truth
> Is often hard to perceive
> We pray that the world
> May be illumined by its light:
> Hypocrisy and falsity exposed;
> Eternal values glimpsed;
> Love's power made known;
> Mindless prejudices dissolved;
> Honesty and goodness,
> Compassion and understanding
> Revealed as the real wisdom
> Allied to the Wisdom of God.

We pray for all those who seek after truth and wisdom, for those who seek God, and for those who share God's word and his love with others.

We pray for all those who shun the truth about themselves, or the realities of suffering and death.

We pray for all those who teach and preach, that they may encourage others to search honestly for what is right throughout their lives.

We pray for ourselves, that we may have the courage to live according to the truths we see in Christ.

Lord, this is our prayer:
*Help us to know and to do your will.*

> You, Lord, are real Life
> And although that life challenges
> Our comfort and complacency
> We pray for your life for the world:
> Life with purpose;
> Life with joy;
> Life with peace;
> Life with adventure;
> Life shared with others
> And with you.

We pray for those who are depressed and anxious, for whom life is a meaningless, agonizing existence.

We pray for those who have been called by God to live in difficult, dangerous or heart-breaking situations.

We pray for those who are lonely or discontent, avoiding life and other people out of distrust and fear.

We pray for ourselves, that we may be filled with the Holy Spirit, and live together in Christ.

Lord, this is our prayer:
*Help us to know and to do your will.*

In Jesus' name, *Amen.*

# Fifth Sunday after Easter

## Going to the Father

L: Lord, send us your Holy Spirit:
R: *That our lives may glorify you.*

Lord,
why is it that this world of yours
is at the mercy of our human limitations,
our blind decision-making, our voracious greed?
We find it hard to understand.
But we pray for those who are the victims
of flawed government,
the victims of their rulers':

>> limited wisdom
>> limited goodness
>> limited justice
>> limited compassion;

victims of their own powerlessness.
We pray that your Spirit may blow in the world,
stirring up the hearts of leaders and people, that
they may be prepared to work and to suffer to create
peaceful and just societies.

Lord, send us your Holy Spirit:
*That our lives may glorify you.*

Lord,
why is it that your family of humankind
have limited their sensitivity and love
by hardening their hearts against one another?
We find it hard to understand.
But we pray for those who are the victims
of our limited love,
the victims of:

famine
intolerance
warfare
poverty;
victims of their need for others.
We pray that your Spirit may inspire the world,
warming up cold hearts so that leaders and people
may be prepared to sacrifice what they do not
really need in order to give others life.

Lord, send us your Holy Spirit:
*That our lives may glorify you.*

Lord,
why do the people of your church,
those who should know and love you best,
often appear lukewarm to others and to you?
We find it hard to understand.
But we pray for those who are the victims
of our reserve:
    the young and the searching
    the stranger in our pew
    those who do not 'fit in'
    our own fellowship;
victims of a timidity about entering real life.
We pray that your Spirit may breathe fresh courage
and assurance into the church, so that leaders and
people may bring the love of God into the lives of
many.

Lord, send us your Holy Spirit:
*That our lives may glorify you.*

Lord,
why is it that the lives of so many
are limited by illness or handicaps,
by faults of character, by early death?
We find it hard to understand.
But we pray for those who are the victims
of such limitations,
those with frustrated lives:
        the sick
        the dying

      those handicapped by physical, mental or emotional
         limitations
      the embittered
      the guilty and regretful
and for all those who love and care for them.

We pray for those who have lost people they love ... and for those who are ill ... or housebound ... We pray, Lord, that your Spirit may come and bring a new sense of freedom into their lives – the freedom that comes from knowing we are loved and accepted by you.

Lord, send us your Holy Spirit:
*That our lives may glorify you.*

In the name of him, who returned to the Father in order that his human limitations might be changed into the freedom of the Holy Spirit, our Risen Lord and Saviour, Jesus Christ, *Amen.*

# Ascension Day

## *The Ascension of Christ*

You are free, Lord,
Your ascension has set you free:
Free from the constraints of human existence,
Outside the limitations of time and space;
Free to be here with us now,
In our worship and fellowship;
For in your freedom
You have bound yourself to us
With a promise,
'Lo, I am with you always,
To the close of the age.'

We pray, Lord, for those
who need to feel you close,
who need the assurance of your love,
the encouragement of your Spirit.
We pray for those who are persecuted
      who are discriminated against
      who are ridiculed
because of their faith or race or colour.

*Silence*

Be with them, Lord.

We pray for those who are imprisoned
      who are tortured
      who are exiled
because they have struggled
for the rights of their people.

*Silence*

Be with them, Lord.

## Ascension Day

We pray for those who are destitute
>who are hungry
>who are refugees
because of the unkindness of our world.

*Silence*

Be with them, Lord.

We pray for those who are filled with guilt
>who are heart-broken
>who are perplexed
because a relationship has gone wrong.

*Silence*

Be with them, Lord.

We pray for those who are feeling fed up
>who are in discomfort
>who are afraid
because they are ill.

*Silence*

Be with them, Lord.

We pray for all those who are numbed
>who are angry
>who are desolate
because they have been bereaved.

*Silence*

Be with them, Lord.

Be with us all, Lord: in our daily struggles to follow you; in our periods of doubt and despair; and in times of happiness, health and loving. Be with us all until the time when in your Kingdom of Love our joy will know no end. *Amen*.

# Sixth Sunday after Easter
## (Sunday after Ascension Day)


### The Ascension of Christ

L: Lord, in your mercy:
R: *Hear our prayer.*

Loving heavenly Father,
In Christ
You have given us new understanding
Of you;
In Christ,
You have given us a message for the world;
In Christ,
You have promised us the power of your Holy Spirit.

We pray
for the nations
to whom we are sent
to preach repentance
and the forgiveness of sins.
We pray
that leaders may repent
of their use of oppression
and of injustice,
of their lack of vision.
We pray
that they may govern
in a continual state of repentance,
forever turning their minds towards
justice, wisdom and compassion;
learning anew
from past mistakes;
building afresh
on new visions.

## Sixth Sunday after Easter

Lord, in your mercy:
*Hear our prayer*

We pray
for the people of the world
to whom we are sent
to preach repentance
and the forgiveness of sins:
that they may repent
of their warring spirit;
of greed exercised
at the cost of poorer lands.
We pray
that they may live
in a continual state of repentance,
forever turning their minds towards
peace, co-operation and co-existence,
using new discoveries
to benefit all peoples;
using past failures
to find future opportunities.

Lord, in your mercy:
*Hear our prayer.*

We pray
for our own nation
to whom we are sent
to preach repentance
and the forgiveness of sins,
that we may all repent of:
> our materialism;
> our racial and class prejudice;
> our apathy.

We pray
that we may live together
in a continual state of repentance,
forever turning our minds towards
the real needs of one another,
giving respect
to every person;
finding new answers
from a history that repeats itself.

Lord, in your mercy:
*Hear our prayer.*

We pray
for the church
that we may fulfil
our mission to preach
repentance and forgiveness
in Christ's name
that we may be one
and bring reconciliation
to the whole world.
We pray
that we may repent of:
       our timidity;
       our insularity;
       our concern for respectability;
       the divisions between us.
We pray
that we may serve together
in a continual state of repentance,
forever turning our minds towards
the Gospel, the world and each other,
that we may bring
hope out of despair;
salvation to those
ignorant of God's love.

Lord, in your mercy:
*Hear our prayer.*

In the name of our Risen Lord and Saviour, Jesus Christ, *Amen.*

# Pentecost
## (Whit Sunday)

### The Gift of the Spirit

L: Spirit of God, breathe into our lives:
R: *Breathe into the church, breathe into the world.*

> We are here, Lord.
> You have brought us here
> And now
> We bring ourselves to you,
> Laying ourselves open
> To your Spirit.
> You know each one of us
> Inside out:
> What we have done;
> What we are;
> Our failures
> And our feelings;
> Our blind spots
> And our talents.
> Let us in silence pray –
> Come, Holy Spirit,
> Breathe forgiveness on us,
> Correct us,
> Strengthen us,
> Use us
> In your love.

> *Silence*

Spirit of God, breathe into our lives:
*Breathe into the church, breathe into the world.*

> We are here, Lord.
> You have brought us here
> And now

We bring to you
Those in need of our prayers:
The sick . . .
The bereaved . . .
The anxious . . .
Come, Holy Spirit
To those in distress,
To those afraid;
Bring comfort,
Bring peace.
Come to us,
When we seek to help,
Guide our words
And the ways
In which we care.

*Silence*

Spirit of God, breathe into our lives:
*Breathe into the church, breathe into the world.*

We are here, Lord.
You have brought us here
And now
We bring to you
The needs of our society
Which seeks new values
And a sense of purpose
In an unstable
And changing world.
Come, Holy Spirit,
Bring neighbourliness
Into our communities,
Bring hope
To our young people,
Bring harmony
Where there is discord.

*Silence*

Spirit of God, breathe into our lives:
*Breathe into the church, breathe into the world.*

We are here, Lord.
You have brought us here
And now
We bring the world to you:
Our world,
Where warfare never ceases;
Our world,
Where millions battle with hunger;
Our world,
Divided between rich North and
Poor South;
Between developed and underdeveloped,
Powerful and powerless;
Split by an Iron Curtain.
Come, Holy Spirit,
Blow down
The barriers that divide us,
Bring us face to face
With those in the world
Who need our concern.

*Silence*

Spirit of God, breathe into our lives:
*Breathe into the church, breathe into the world.*

We are here, Lord.
You have brought us here
As your church.
Your Holy Spirit
Has breathed into us
And given us a message
For the whole earth:
A message of hope,
Of love and forgiveness,
Of joy and salvation,
Of peace.
Come, Holy Spirit,
Fill us up with your love,
Bind us to God,
Bind us together,
Make each one of us
Complete in you.

*Silence*

Spirit of God, breathe into our lives:
*Breathe into the church, breathe into the world.*

We pray through the Spirit, in gratitude to God and in the name of our Lord Jesus Christ, *Amen*.

# Trinity Sunday
## (1st Sunday after Pentecost)

### 1. The Riches of God

Lord, we pray for ourselves
and for all people
that the poverty of our lives
may be transformed
by the riches of your grace.
For we know
that much of the poverty
of our world
springs from what is lacking
in the hearts of humankind.

Lord, we are poor in wisdom,
in understanding and vision.
We cannot discern
how it would be
if the world were ordered
according to your design.
We see justice and compassion
as the ideal ways of ruling
in an ideal world
and not as the true ways
the right ways
the pragmatic ways
that they are,
because they fulfil
your purposes and your destiny
for humankind.

Lord, we are poor in understanding.
We pray that you will graciously enrich us with your true wisdom.

Lord, we are poor in love.
All our relationships
are impoverished by our selfishness.
The whole world
is impoverished by our greed.
We long for a love
that is totally satisfying,
that draws us on
and makes us whole,
yet the demands
such love would make
frighten us deeply:
in a world of such need
what might we not be asked?
So we fence ourselves in,
create an illusion of safety,
deny our own poverty,
turn our backs on you.

Lord, we are poor in love.
We pray that you will graciously forgive us and enrich us with your
never-ending love.

Lord, we are poor in faith.
Our lack of trust in you
and our lack of courage
mean that we deny ourselves
the riches of real life in you;
mean that we deny this hope
to other people.
We pray for the faithful
who continue to speak out
in word and action
to a shifting society:
people may listen
or they may not,
but the words resound
to your glory.

Lord, we are poor in faith.
We pray that you will so graciously enrich us that we may live by
faith in you.

Lord, we are poor in gratitude.
We belong to you.
We believe that you
are a suffering, self-giving God
who will go to any lengths
to gain our love
and give us life.
We live in a society
where the necessities for physical life
can always be obtained.
Yet the attitude of thankfulness
is foreign to many of us.
We perceive ourselves as poor,
when we are very rich,
and our faulty perception
stints our generosity
with money, with time,
with our lives.

Lord, we are poor in gratitude.
We ask that you will graciously impress us with the abundance of
your gifts to us, that our hearts may be glad and thankful.

Lord, we are poor in spirit,
and though we sometimes pretend
we can make it on our own,
we need you.
We need you to surround us
with your love.
We need you with us,
giving us peace.
We need you beside us
to lift us when we fall.
We need you ahead of us
to guide us.
We need you behind us,
pushing us on.

Lord, we are poor in spirit.
We are blessed, for we know our need of you.
We pray that the riches of your grace may be poured out upon us
and that we may live in you.

In the name of him who was rich, but for our sakes became poor,
our Lord Jesus Christ, *Amen.*

# Trinity Sunday
## (First Sunday after Pentecost)

### 2. The Church's Message

L: Lord, in your mercy:
R: *Hear our prayer.*

~~We have a message~~.
We have a message of peace:
~~Inner peace~~
from the knowledge of God's love;
Peace in our communities
from love for one another;
Peace in the world
from a shared concern for ~~humankin~~d. *humanity*

Lord, we pray
for all those who bring
your message of peace:
for those in the church
who preach and teach
of your forgiveness;
for those within communities
who work to reconcile,
to break down barriers
of fear and distrust;
for those who campaign
for peace for the world
~~and for those~~ who negotiate
treaties and settlements.

Lord, in your mercy:
*Hear our prayer.*

~~We have a message.~~
We have a message of hope:
~~Hope for the faithful~~

that God will see us through;
Hope for our communities
that someone will always champion
the disadvantaged and oppressed;
Hope for the world
in the discovery
of our need for one another.

Lord, we pray
for all those who bring
your message of hope:
for those engaged
in the church's ministry~~, to~~
~~for those who~~ bring comfort
and a new vision
to the destitute;
for those who work
amongst the starving,
implementing policies
for tomorrow, as well as today.

Lord, in your mercy:
*Hear our prayer.*

~~We have a message.~~
We have a message of life:
life triumphant over death and sickness;
~~life triumphant over suffering and sorrow;~~
~~Life for those~~
~~who live in Chr~~ist;
~~life for communities~~
~~once cold and barren~~;
life for the world
in the promise
of God's redemption.

Lord, we pray
for all those who bring
your message of life,
those who make the
Resurrection of Christ
a reality today:
for members of the church
whose caring lives

~~in past ages~~
~~and in the present~~
witness to Christ's triumph;
for all those who care
for the suffering;
~~for those whose insight~~
~~and enthusiastic work~~
~~put new heart~~
~~into dying communities;~~
for all those who work
for the coming of God's kingdom
of life and love and joy.

Lord, in your mercy:
*Hear our prayer.*

We have a message.
We have the good news
that God was in Christ
reconciling
the world to himself.
Lord, may the church
be united in you,
that we may be
effective messengers
of your healing love
for all ~~humankind~~. *Amen*.
*humanity.*

# Second Sunday after Pentecost
## (Trinity 1)

## 1. The People of God

L: Lord, we are your own people:
R: *Call us, guide us, keep us.*

Lord God,
we are a people
with a common identity,
Christians named
after your Son.
We have a common life
yet no one country
but the Promised Land
of your love.
We believe that the whole earth is yours,
our home is the world,
our motherland has no boundaries.

Lord, we pray for your world-wide church. As we are one in
Christ, so may we share a common concern for areas of need
throughout the world, and a common mission to take God's love
to the ends of the earth. We pray for all those from this country
who are working for the church overseas (for . . . ) and for
those who have come from other lands to work and share with us
(for . . . )

Lord, we are your own people:
*Call us, guide us, keep us.*

Lord God,
we are your people,
but there is no language
uniquely ours.
Your praises are sung
in every nation,

in many tongues.
But you have given us
a gospel message
for the whole world:
Words of love,
    of forgiveness,
    of comfort,
    of hope;
words that speak
to the hearts
of humankind.

Lord, we pray for your world-wide church, that we may never be too afraid to own you our Lord and Master. We pray for all those who are persecuted for speaking out about their faith (for . . . ). We pray for all preachers and teachers of the gospel and for all those engaged in bringing words of comfort to the sick and distressed (for . . . ).

Lord, we are your own people:
*Call us, guide us, keep us.*

Lord God,
we are your people
and we use the customs
of our own society
in our search for
morality and truth;
Yet the customs
of the people of God
are to be found
in every place:
the custom of worship
the custom of the sacraments
the custom of self-giving love.

Lord, we pray for the world-wide church, that there may be a spirit of love and respect between Christians of different nations and cultures. We pray for the worship in our churches, that it might be enthusiastic yet reverent, simple yet meaningful, symbolic yet relevant. We pray for ourselves, as we seek to work out in our everyday lives the meaning of a Christian life.

Lord, we are your people:
*Call us, guide us, keep us.*

Lord God,
we are your people
but no external appearance
marks us out:
we are of all colours;
we are of all ages;
we are men and women;
we wear lounge suits,
      saris, cassocks,
      loincloths, kaftans;
we are rich
and we are poor.

Lord, we pray for the world-wide church, that our arms may be
held open to all people, of every colour, class or race and that we
may show no partiality towards those whom our society finds most
admirable. We ask that the appearance of every Christian may
reflect that of Christ, in loving attitudes, right-living and self-
sacrifice.

Lord, we are your people:
*Call us, guide us, keep us.*

Lord God,
we are your people
and like other peoples
we have our own
history and traditions.
In every new generation
you bring to new life
the truths that we learn
from the Bible.
In every new generation
children are born
who will speak your word
for their time.

We pray for the world-wide church and for all those who translate
and preach and teach from the scriptures, that God's word may be
passed on. We pray that we may learn from the church's history
and from the times when the church has failed in its task of love so
that we may gain new wisdom from past mistakes. We thank God
for all those Christians throughout the ages whose lives have been

beacons of truth to the world, giving thanks especially for those whom we have known (for . . . ).

Lord, we are your people:
*Call us, guide us, keep us.*

In the name of Jesus Christ, the leader and Saviour of his people, *Amen*.

# Second Sunday after Pentecost
*(Trinity 1)*

## 2. The Church's Unity and Fellowship

L: In our love for others and our life together:
R: *Lord, make us one in you.*

Lord, we pray for own church here in ... We thank you for its
fellowship and ask that your Holy Spirit may continually lead us
into deeper communion with one another. May you guide us in all
that we do (and especially ). ... We pray that our desire to love
and serve you may over-ride any differences and disagreements
between us. We bring before you those from within our church for
whom we are particularly concerned. We pray for ... and ask that
they may be comforted and strengthened by the knowledge of
your presence and of our love and care.)

In our love for others and our life together:
*Lord, make us one in you.*

Lord, we pray for all the churches in our neighbourhood, their
work and witness, for ... (names of churches) and for their
ministers (priests/vicars/etc.) ... and people. We ask that you will
draw all Christians in this area into a deeper sense of unity with
one another, as we seek to meet the needs of the community in
which we live. (We pray for ... )

In our love for others and our life together:
*Lord, make us one in you.*

Lord, we pray for the churches throughout our land, ministering in
many different situations; each situation with its own opportunities
and problems. We pray for congregations in rural areas, in
suburbia, in council estates, in inner cities, in town centres. We
remember the work of the various chaplaincies, in hospitals,
educational establishments, penal institutions, industries and the
armed forces. (We pray for ... ) May we, too, share in the

nationwide work of the church by showing interest and concern
and by offering the support of our money and our prayers.

In our love for others and our life together:
*Lord, make us one in you.*

Lord, we pray for the worldwide church. We pray for those from
this country who have gone to serve overseas (for . . . ) and
for those who have come from other countries to share with us
(for . . . ). We ask that as in this age of communication we have
come to learn much more about the many peoples of our world
and their way of life, so may we, as Christians, come to discover a
deeper sense of oneness with Christians throughout the world. We
pray that the knowledge of our unity in Christ may show itself in
the practical way of caring for those in need.

In our love for others and our life together:
*Lord, make us one in you.*

We thank you, Lord, that in you we are one with Christians
throughout the ages and we remember, with joy, the lives of those
who lived and died in the faith we share. We praise you with the
whole family of the church in every place, on earth and in heaven,
making our prayers in the name of Jesus Christ, our Lord and
Saviour. *Amen.*

# Third Sunday after Pentecost
*(Trinity 2)*

## 1. The Life of the Baptized

> Lord,
> in baptism
> we are promised
> newness of life
> in you.

Lord, we pray for all those
whose lives are a struggle
for mere existence,
who have lost the capacity
to live full lives,
who have no inner peace.
We pray for those
who are destitute or starving;
those forced to work
in inhuman conditions
for long, dreary hours.
We pray for those
who have enough to live on
but whose expectations
of the 'good life'
drive them relentlessly
to work for more things,
leaving no time
for the blossoming of true happiness.

*Silence*

Lord, we ask for newness of life for the world.
Help us to feed, with bread and with spiritual food, all those who
hunger for life.

Lord, we pray for all those
whose lives are regarded
as being of little importance,
who find themselves denigrated,
neglected or unfairly used.
We pray for those
whose dignity as human beings
has been taken away
along with their human rights.
We pray for those
oppressed in their powerlessness,
the victims of injustice
because they are black,
or because they are poor,
or because they believe in you.
We pray for those in our society
who feel that they are treated
with condescension.

*Silence*

Lord, we ask for newness of life for the world.
Help us to place real value on every human life given by you and to
show that love in our words, our actions and in generous giving.

Lord, we pray for all those
who see their own lives
as empty and without purpose.
We pray for those who are depressed
and cannot see any light
at the end of their black tunnel.
We pray for those who feel
that their lives are valueless
because they are old
or sick or unemployed.
We pray for those
who despise themselves
because of what they are
or have done
and for those who have lost their faith in you
and can find no meaning
for life or for the world.

*Silence*

141

Lord we ask for newness of life for the world.
Help us to show, in our lives, the joy and sense of purpose that
come from following you and help us to offer to others, in our
patient listening and understanding, a glimpse of new hope
founded on your love and acceptance.

Lord, we pray for all those
who are finding their lives
painful, confusing and hard:
for those who are ill
... (or *silence*)
for those with anxieties
... (or *silence*)
for those who have been bereaved
... (or *silence*)
and for all those who are lonely or afraid,
sorrowful or exhausted.

Lord, we ask for newness of life for the world.
We pray that those who are suffering may find comfort and healing
in the knowledge of your ever-present love and through our care
and concern.

We make our prayers as part of our common life of worship and
service in Christ Jesus our Lord, *Amen.*

# Third Sunday after Pentecost
*(Trinity 2)*

## 2. The Church's Confidence in Christ

L: Loving Lord, the Rock of our Salvation:
R: *Give us the confidence to build on you.*

Lord,
upon what shall we build our lives?
shall we place our confidence
in governments?
in their protection? in their compassion?
in their power?
Lord, we remember before you
all those whose lives have been ruined
by the governments set over them:
those needing protection
against government injustice;
those needing compassion
because of government neglect;
those killed or maimed or injured
in their government's thirst for power.

Loving Lord, the Rock of our Salvation:
*Give us the confidence to build on you.*

Lord,
upon what shall we build our lives?
shall we place all our confidence
in the love of family and friends?
in being needed? in popularity?
in the return of affection?
Lord, we remember before you
all those whose lives have been shattered
because of the limitations of human love:
those whose need to be needed
has turned into ~~poisonous~~ possessiveness;

those whose search for popularity
has led them to hide their real selves;
those who feel that their love has been wasted
on those who no longer care.

Living Lord, the Rock of our Salvation:
*Give us the confidence to build on you.*

Lord,
upon what shall we build our lives?
shall we place our confidence
in the Church which you founded?
in church attendance? in the Bible?
in good deeds?
Lord, we remember before you
all those whose lives have been stunted
by their reliance on the externals of faith:
for those who have heard words of comfort at church
but have closed their ears to the words of challenge;
for those who have turned the Bible
into written Law
and limited the work of the Spirit
in their minds and hearts and lives;
for those whose good deeds bring cold satisfaction
and not the warmth of love into their hearts.

Loving Lord, the Rock of our Salvation:
*Give us the confidence to build on you.*

Lord,
upon what shall we build our lives?
shall we place our confidence in ourselves?
and our achievements?
in our wealth? in our talents?
in our independence?
Lord, we remember before you
all those whose lives are destitute
because they rely only on themselves:
those who have worked all hours for money
but have lost the love of partner and children;
those who have found that their talents
have not brought fulfilment to their lives;
those whose life-long avoidance of commitment
has left them alienated and alone.

144

Loving Lord, the Rock of our Salvation:
*Give us the confidence to build on you.*

Lord,
we shall build our lives on you.
We shall place our confidence in Christ
and in his saving love. *Amen.*

# Fourth Sunday after Pentecost
*(Trinity 3)*

✓

## 1. The Freedom of the Children of God

L: Lord, hear us:
*R: Lord, graciously hear us.*

Let us pray:
Lord, we pray for those enslaved ~~Caught up~~
by unjust, ~~corrupt~~ and uncaring governments; *and*
~~for those who are treated as little better than slaves~~
by oppressive and materialistic societies.
We remember before you
All those who struggle
To bring freedom to these peoples.
We ask that your Spirit
May guide and inspire them
~~So that one form of bondage~~
~~Is not replaced by another.~~

~~Lord, we pray that oppressed peoples may find the glorious~~
~~freedom you give to your children.~~

Lord, hear us:
*Lord, graciously hear us.*

Lord, we pray for those enslaved
~~by the precariousness of their existence~~:
~~those who are slaves~~
to hunger, thirst ~~and malnutrition~~;
~~those who are slaves~~
to homelessness, cold and disease;
~~those whose lives are held captive~~
~~by the threat of warfare and violence~~.
We remember before you
All those who work
To bring freedom to these people:

146

To feed them today,
And give them hope for tomorrow;
To bring the security of peace
To our troubled world.

Lord, we pray that those whose lives are under threat may find the
glorious freedom you give to your children.

Lord, hear us:
*Lord, graciously hear us.*

Lord, we pray for those enslaved
by their own fear and greed and blindness: desire
those whose lives and whose potential
are stunted by fear of rejection and failure;
those whose time is spent acquiring possessions
that seem of little worth once possessed;
those so blinkered by ignorance and prejudice self
that they miss the joy to be found
in communion with others and with you.
We remember before you
All those whom you call
To bring freedom to these people,
To break down the barriers
Between one person and another,
Between people and Life,
Between people and you.

Lord, we pray for those enslaved by their own weaknesses, that
they may find the glorious freedom you give to your children.

Lord, hear us:
*Lord, graciously hear us.*

Lord, we pray for those enslaved
by physical or mental suffering:
for those whose lives are overshadowed
by the pain caused by illness or injury;
for those whose lives are held captive
by anxiety, depression or grief.
We remember before you
All those who are concerned
To bring freedom to these people,
To bring healing and comfort,
To listen and to care,
To convey hope.

Lord, we pray that all suffering people may find the glorious freedom that you give to your children.

Lord, hear us:
*Lord, graciously hear us.*

In the name of our Saviour, Jesus Christ, who broke the bonds of sin and death, *Amen*.

# Fourth Sunday after Pentecost
## (Trinity 3)

## 2. The Church's Mission to the Individual

L: Lord, this is our prayer:
R: *Help us to know and to do your will.*

Lord,
here is a person
who is looking for you.
He knows you by name
and by reputation
but longs to meet you
face to face;
to see you at work
in the world
and in his life.

Lord, we pray that he may find you.

Lord, this is our prayer:
*Help us to know and to do your will.*

Lord,
here is a person
who is trying to ignore you,
whose unease about her life
is not something
she wishes to face.
She is sceptical
about that joy and love
that belief in you
is supposed to bring.

Lord, we pray that your love may break through to her.

Lord, this is our prayer:
*Help us to know and to do your will.*

Lord,
here is a person
who knows you only
as all-seeing Judge;
who hates himself
and is riddled with guilt;
who lives in regret
of past actions and words;
who lives in despair
of ever finding peace.

Lord, we pray that he might find peace in accepting your
forgiveness.

Lord, this is our prayer:
*Help us to know and to do your will.*

Lord,
here is a person
who is glad to know
that you are like her,
respectable and, on the whole,
conservative in tastes;
ready to cushion her
against life's blows,
protect her from life's changes.

Lord, we pray that you will surprise her, meeting her where she
least expected you to be.

Lord, this is our prayer:
*Help us to know and to do your will.*

Lord,
here is a person
who needs you
but feels that you
are far away;
who is ill and anxious,
afraid of death;
who, in his anguish
feels desperately alone.

Lord, we pray that he may become aware of your constant, loving
presence.

Lord, this is our prayer:
*Help us to know and to do your will.*

Lord,
here is a person
who is angry with you,
who believes that you
have done nothing to stop
the death of someone
she deeply loves;
who cannot see
why pain and death
exist in your world.

Lord, we pray that she may find release in the knowledge that she
does not weep alone, for you weep with her.

Lord, this is our prayer:
*Help us to know and to do your will.*

Lord,
here are we,
your church.
We ask that you
will fill us with your Spirit
that we may be faithful and effective
messengers of your love
for all humankind.

Lord, this is our prayer:
*Help us to know and to do your will. Amen.*

# Fifth Sunday after Pentecost
*(Trinity 4)*

## 1. The New Law

L: Lord, guide and strengthen us with your Spirit:
*R: That we may obey your law of love.*

Lord,
we remember before you
those countries ruled by laws
that contradict your law of love;
those countries ruled by laws
that are unjust or unwise
and we pray
for those in badly ruled lands
whose obedience to you
results in a dangerous struggle
to change the law.
(We pray for . . . )

Lord, guide and strengthen us with your Spirit:
*That we may obey your law of love.*

Lord,
we remember before you
our own society whose laws
attempt to protect the unfortunate
but where, despite the welfare state
there is still need of every kind.
The old, the young, the sick
and those unable to cope with life
are hungry for care and concern
and we pray
for those who, in obedience to you
care for and champion
the powerless in our society

and work amongst those
whom society has failed.
(We pray for . . . )

Lord, guide and strengthen us with your Spirit:
*That we may obey your law of love.*

Lord,
we remember before you the church,
called upon to show the standards
for Christian moral life
in a world of shifting moral values,
yet also called to follow
the dictates of love alone
rather than the letter of moral law
and we pray
for every individual Christian
and for church representatives
as they debate and discuss Christian attitudes
to the moral issues of our day.
(We pray for . . . )

Lord, guide and strengthen us with your Spirit:
*That we may obey your law of love.*

Lord,
we bring to you
our own dilemmas
about the ways
in which we live our lives.
We ask you to extend
our view of what is right
beyond the law, beyond
our own personal morality
into an attitude of love
towards the whole world.
We pray
that we may keep close to you
so that you can inform
our decisions and our care.
We pray for the coming
of your kingdom of love.

*Fifth Sunday after Pentecost*

Lord, guide and strengthen us with your Spirit:
*That we may obey your law of love.*

In Jesus' name, *Amen*.

# Fifth Sunday after Pentecost
## *(Trinity 4)*


### 2. *The Church's Mission to all the World*

L: Lord, in your mercy:
*R: Hear our prayer.*

'Go out!
Go out into the world!'

But, Lord,
we want to stay here.
We're happy in fellowship
here together.
We know one another.
We share together.
We care for one another.
We're living
perfectly adequate
Christian lives
just as we are.
Why go out
into a world of strangers?
Why share
with those we don't know?
Why care
for those who might misunderstand?

Lord, we pray
that your Spirit might convince us
that your love is to be shared
with all,
that your salvation
is for the world.
We ask that you will equip us
with hearts overflowing

with your good news,
with courage
and with resolution.

Lord, in your mercy:
*Hear our prayer.*

'Go out!
Go out with my message!'

Lord,
we are a people of words,
of pious phrases:
we can speak
of sin, repentance, forgiveness,
redemption and salvation,
atonement and justification,
but how can you expect us
to say these words,
which we scarcely understand,
to those
who have never heard them?

Lord, we pray
that your Spirit will give us
the right words to use:
words of friendship and comfort;
words of concern and love;
words of joy and peace;
words that challenge,
provoke a deep response;
words of good news,
words of God.

Lord, in your mercy:
*Hear our prayer.*

'Go out!
Go, tell everyone!'

Everyone, Lord?
We know that
your love is for all
but surely you should send
someone else
to show it to those people

who are different from us;
someone who understands
their way of life,
the words they use;
someone who wouldn't
put their foot in it
like we would.

Lord, we pray
that your Spirit will enable us
to break down the barriers
that separate us from one another
so that we may bring
your healing love
into the lives
of the peoples of our world.

Lord, in your mercy:
*Hear our prayer*.

In the name of him who died for us all, Jesus Christ our Lord and Saviour, *Amen*.

# Sixth Sunday after Pentecost
## (Trinity 5)

### The New Humanity

L: The Lord hears our prayer:
*R: Thanks be to God.*

Lord, we want to be
your new people.
We want our ~~lives,~~ hopes
        ~~our hopes~~
        and our vision to be
constantly renewed by you.
We want our lives to be
full of the freshness
and the goodness
that spring from
the thankfulness and joy
your Spirit inspires.

The Lord hears our prayer:
*Thanks be to God.*

Lord,
as your new people
we will work and pray
for the renewing
of this ~~battle-worn earth~~. world.
We ask that the vision
of your new kingdom
of justice, love and peace
may be kept fresh in the minds
of leaders and people alike.
(We pray for . . . )

The Lord hears our prayer:
*Thanks be to God.*

Lord,
as your new people
we will work and pray
for the renewing
of our ~~depressed society~~. Church + society.
We ask that your Spirit
may stir up our hearts to recognise your glory + beauty. + love
with new hopes for the future; that you would open our eyes to
may open our eyes      the spiritual possibilities ~~draw~~
to new horizons                      around us.
of integrity and care. that you would call us into a
(We pray for ... ) deeper and more loving relationship with
                                 you.
The Lord hears our prayer:
*Thanks be to God.*

Lord,
as your new people
we will work and pray
for the renewing
of other people's lives.
We ask that you
will be with those
who are ill or sorrowful,
anxious or bereaved,
healing, uplifting,
comforting and reassuring them.
(We pray for ... )

The Lord hears our prayer:
*Thanks be to God.*

Lord, in you all things are made new. In you, we can become the
sort of people you mean us to be. We ask that ~~in the power of your
Holy Spir~~it we may turn away from the old sin that kept us from
you and be filled with new life in Christ, in whose name we pray,
*Amen.*

# Seventh Sunday after Pentecost
## *(Trinity 6)*

*The More Excellent Way*

Lord, we have faith in you.
We trust you implicitly, with our lives.
Lord, we hope in you alone,
for you alone will never fail us.

Lord, because you love us
we love you,
we love your world,
we love one another,
we love ourselves
and we pray that you will
so increase our love
that the world which we serve
may have faith and hope in you.

*Silence*

In love,
let us pray for the world,
that love may prevail:
    love that feeds the hungry;
    love that defends the weak;
    love that loves fairly;
    love that returns right for wrong;
    love that brings peace.    → we especially prayfor.

*Silence*

In love,
let us pray for those who suffer,
that love may prevail:
    love that heals the sick;
    love that stays with the dying;

love that comforts the sorrowful;
love that calms the fearful;
love that suffers with us. → we remember the sick + especially

*Silence*

In love
let us pray for the whole church of God
that love may prevail:
    love that binds all Christians together;
    love that inspires our worship;
    love that is sensitive to need;
    love that is humble and kind;
    love that reaches out to all. we pray for our church or diocesan

*Silence*

In love,
let us pray for ourselves, In love let us pray for anything else
that love may prevail:
    love that overcomes fear;
    love that brings understanding;
    love that is motivated by another's needs;
    love that gives everything;
    love that is of God.

*Silence*

Lord, we pray that our love may bear all things, believe all things,
hope all things, endure all things, so that our lives may be
reflections of your love and give glory to you.

In the name of Jesus Christ, *Amen.*

# Eighth Sunday after Pentecost
*(Trinity 7)*

## The Fruit of the Spirit

L: Lord, make us one in the Spirit:
*R: That the church may bear your fruit.*

The fruit of the Spirit is love.
We bring before God a world corrupted
by injustice, indifference and hatred –
a world in need of love.

*(Silence)*

Lord, make us one in the Spirit:
*That the church may bear your fruit.*

The fruit of the Spirit is joy.
We bring before God a sorrowing world
full of despair and suffering –
a world in need of joy.

*(Silence)*

Lord, make us one in the Spirit:
*That the church may bear your fruit.*

The fruit of the Spirit is peace.
We bring before God a world torn apart
by warfare and inner conflict –
a world in need of peace.

*(Silence)*

Lord, make us one in the Spirit:
*That the church may bear your fruit.*

The fruit of the Spirit is patience.
We bring before God a world damaged
by humankind's short-term perspective –
a world in need of patience.

*(Silence)*

Lord, make us one in the Spirit:
*That the church may bear your fruit.*

The fruit of the Spirit is kindness.
We bring before God a world made cruel
by insensitivity and violence –
a world in need of kindness.

*(Silence)*

Lord, make us one in the Spirit:
*That the church may bear your fruit.*

The fruit of the Spirit is goodness.
We bring before God a world made cynical
by the wrongs of humankind –
a world in need of goodness.

*(Silence)*

Lord, make us one in the Spirit:
*That the church may bear your fruit.*

The fruit of the Spirit is faithfulness.
We bring before God a world emptied of meaning
through lack of purpose and belief –
a world in need of faith.

*(Silence)*

Lord, make us one in the Spirit:
*That the church may bear your fruit.*

The fruit of the Spirit is gentleness.
We bring before God a world that seems harsh
towards weakness and need –
a world in need of gentleness.

*(Silence)*

Lord, make us one in the Spirit:
*That the church may bear your fruit.*

The fruit of the Spirit is self-control.
We bring before God a world enslaved
by greed and lust and violence –
a world in need of self-control.

### Eighth Sunday after Pentecost

*(Silence)*

Lord, make us one in the Spirit:
*That the church may bear your fruit.*

Lord, we pray that your holy Spirit may rule the hearts and minds
of your people so that the world may glimpse within the church the
redemption for which it yearns.

In the Saviour's name, *Amen.*

# Ninth Sunday after Pentecost
## (Trinity 8)

*The Whole Armour of God*

L: Lord, give us the light armour of faith:
*R: That we may face all with you.*

Lord, we all
feel the need
to protect ourselves
against the knocks of life,
against hurts inflicted by others.

We each make
a suit of armour
to protect ourselves
and we know that it is there
because it weighs us down.

Lord, give us the light armour of faith:
*That we may face all with you.*

We make for ourselves
the armour of indifference
that we may not share
in the sufferings of others,
may not hear the cries
of the hungry and distressed,
need not give our money,
our time or ourselves.
But our thick armour
isolates us from others,
cuts us off from the Christ
who is found in those in need.

Lord, we pray for all those
who arm themselves with indifference
who neglect others
and isolate themselves.

Lord, give us the light armour of faith:
*That we may face all with you.*

We make for ourselves
the armour of conservatism
that we might feel secure
in the ways and thinking
of times that are past;
so that we need not face
the demands of the present
or the realities of change.
But our leaden armour
leaves us confused
by the world we see,
makes faith seem brittle
and the future dark.

Lord, we pray for all those
who arm themselves with conservatism,
who neglect the needs of the present age,
who are bereft of a vision.

Lord, give us the light armour of faith:
*That we may face all with you.*

We make for ourselves
the armour of possessions
that our lives may be secure
in a hostile, changing world,
that we may gain respect,
despite our hidden weaknesses
and our lack of self-worth.
But our hard-earned armour
can leave us emotionally poor
and spiritually bankrupt,
unable to rely on
the free gift of God's grace.

Lord, we pray for all those
who arm themselves with possessions,
who neglect the real needs
of others and of themselves.

Lord, give us the light armour of faith:
*That we may face all with you.*

Lord, we make for ourselves suits of armour out of our own fears
and weaknesses. We arm ourselves with popularity, with shyness,
with pride. But when times of trial and temptation come, we find
that none of these enables us to cope with the blows, for they set
up barriers between us and other people, between us and you.

Lord, give us the light armour of faith:
*That we may face all with you.*

Lord, we pray for all those who need your armour of faith today.
We remember those who are experiencing difficulties in their lives
and pray for . . . We pray for all who are persecuted for their faith
and for all who minister to others at peril of their own lives,
freedom, or health.

Lord, give us the light armour of faith:
*That we may face all with you.*

We make our prayers in the name of Christ, our Captain and our
Leader. *Amen.*

# Tenth Sunday after Pentecost
*(Trinity 9)*

## The Mind of Christ ⟨silence⟩

L: Lord, in your mercy:
*R: Hear our prayer.*

Lord, we pray for the church here in . . .
that we may be one,
being of the same mind
as Christ Jesus, our Lord.

Lord, in your mercy:
*Hear our prayer.*

Let us pray for all those who have positions of responsibility within
our church community:
    for the minister
    for preachers
    for class leaders
    for the leaders of fellowship meetings
    for pastoral visitors
    for Sunday School (Junior Church) teachers
    for youth leaders
    for church stewards
    for stewards of property and finance
Lord, we ask that we may remain aware that in Christ we are
servants of one another and of you. Help us all to fulfil our duties
faithfully and well. *to serve with joy and with love.*

Lord, in your mercy:
*Hear our prayer.*

Let us pray for the fellowship and spiritual growth of our church
community:
    for the areas of conflict and tension
    for those who do not feel they belong
    for the deepening of commitment to one another

for a greater sharing of faith
for fuller, richer acts of worship
for a vision for the future.

Lord, we ask that through our humble sharing of life and worship with one another, we may together grow into the full glory of Christian maturity.

Lord, in your mercy:
*Hear our prayer.*

Let us pray for those from within our church who are sad or who are suffering:

for those ill in mind or body
for . . .
for those who have been bereaved
for . . .
for those filled with anxiety
for . . .
for those facing changes in their lives
for . . .

Lord, we ask that in you we may be one with one another and so bear one another's burdens with courage and love.

Lord, in your mercy:
*Hear our prayer.*

Let us pray for the world which the church is called to serve with the self-giving love of Christ:

for the people with whom we come into daily contact
for . . .
for the community in which we live
for . . .
for our troubled society
for . . .
for those in other countries who need our help, interest and
support
for . . .

Lord, we ask that in all we do we may seek to meet the needs of others, and not only our own needs and desires.

Lord, in your mercy:
*Hear our prayer.*

Lord, we pray for
the whole church of God

### Tenth Sunday after Pentecost

throughout the world *especially*
and here in ...  —→ *diocesan prayer.*
that we may all be one,
being of the same mind
as Christ Jesus our Lord.

Lord, in your mercy:
*Hear our prayer.*

In the name of him who emptied himself of all but love to become
our Risen and Adored Lord, Jesus Christ, *Amen.*

# Eleventh Sunday after Pentecost
## (Trinity 10)

### The Serving Community

Lord,
you showed yourself,
in Christ, our humble Saviour,
to be a servant God;
and you call us to be
a servant people,
servant to the whole world.

Lord, show us how we can serve your world.

*Silence*

In Christ
you showed yourself
servant God
to those in need:
you fed those hungry
in body and soul
and you taught your followers
to do the same.

Lord, teach us how we can serve the needy.

*Silence*

In Christ
you showed yourself
servant God
to the ill and distressed;
you gave healing and comfort
and you have given
the Spirit of healing love
to your followers.

Lord, show us how we can serve the sick and the sorrowful.

## Eleventh Sunday after Pentecost

*Silence*

In Christ
you showed yourself
to be a servant God.
You were a messenger
of truth and hope,
preaching to all
who needed Good News
and by your Spirit
you founded the church
that the Gospel might be
passed on for all time.

Lord, show us how we can serve those who seek after truth and
meaning.

*Silence*

In Christ
you showed yourself
as servant God
even to those whom
respectable society rejected.
You were a friend
to tax collectors
and to prostitutes;
you touched and healed
the leprous and insane
And you told your followers
that what they do
for the least of humankind
they do for you.

Lord, show us how to serve those outcast by our society.

*Silence*

In Christ
you showed yourself
to be a servant God.
You washed the feet
of your own disciples
and called them friends.
You instructed them

172

to do for one another
what you had done
for them.

Lord, show us how best to serve one another.

*Silence*

In Christ
you showed yourself
to be a servant God.
You took up
the cross of suffering
to show us
that there is no limit
to your love
and you called
for your followers
to be ready to do the same.

Lord, show us how we can give ourselves in order to serve others
and to serve you.

*Silence*

Lord, we thank you
that we are not only your servants
but are called your children,
heirs to your kingdom of love and joy
through Christ Jesus
our servant, brother and Lord. *Amen*.

# Twelfth Sunday after Pentecost
## *(Trinity 11)*

### The Witnessing Community

L: Lord, we offer you our deeds, our words and our lives:
*R: That we may be witnesses to your love.*

Lord, we pray for the church
and for its caring action
that witnesses to your love.
We pray for those Christians
working with people
in countries overseas *and in this country*
to alleviate poverty, hunger,
ignorance and disease.
We pray for those Christians
in this country
working with those
who are lonely, ill,
distressed or in need.
We remember the work:
       of the Overseas Division
       and of the inner city missions
       and of all church charities.

Lord, we offer you our deeds, our words and our lives:
*That we may be witnesses to your love.*

Lord, we pray for the churches here in . . .
and for their caring action
that witnesses to your love.
We pray for those of us
whose daily work
involves caring for others.
We pray for those involved
in trying to meet the needs
of the people in this area.

174

We pray for all the activities
of this church community,
for its pastoral care
of the sick and the troubled. . . . .
We pray for those actions
that form part of our worship,
that convey in symbol and gesture
God's love for all:
the welcoming handshake;
the baptism of an infant;
our sharing together
at the table of the Lord.

Lord, we offer you our deeds, our words and our lives:
*That we be witnesses to your love.*

Lord, we pray for the church
and for its caring words
that witness to your love.
We pray for Christians
engaged in mission and outreach
in countries overseas
and amongst the people of this land.
We pray that they may humbly
bring the light of your Gospel
to bear on the thoughts and lives
of those who hear their words.
We pray for all those
who give new words and thoughts
to the church:
for theologians and those who write
on pastoral care or for devotional use;
for those who study and update
the words of our faith and worship
to make them words for today.

Lord, we offer you our deeds, our words and our lives:
*That we may be witnesses to your love.*

Lord, we pray for the churches here in . . .
and for their caring words
that witness to your love.
We pray for our ministers and preachers,
for our teachers and leaders

who preach and teach
the Gospel Word.
We pray for those called upon
to bring words of comfort and hope,
of love and concern
to those who are ill,
afraid or bereaved.
We pray that we may all
find the right opportunities
and the right words
to speak of the joy and peace
offered to all in Christ.

Lord, we offer you our deeds, our words and our lives:
*That we may be witnesses to your love.*

Lord, we pray for your church,
for all Christians, everywhere,
that we may be one with them
your followers throughout the ages
whose ways of living and dying
have witnessed to your love.
We pray that
> our church life together
> our personal priorities
> our family life
> our political involvement
> our use of money
> our attitude to others
> our attitude to work

may all be effective witnesses to the Gospel of Christ,
to his way of self-giving, suffering love,
to the triumph of his resurrection,
and to the faith that nothing can separate us
from God's love.

Lord, we offer you our deeds, our words and our lives:
*That we may be witnesses to your love.*

In Christ's name, *Amen.*

176

# Thirteenth Sunday after Pentecost
*(Trinity 12)*

## The Suffering Community

L: Lord, in your mercy:
R: *Hear our prayer.*

Lord,
here is a follower of Christ
who is suffering:
he is persecuted
because he believes in you;
he is afraid
for himself
and for those he loves.

Lord, we pray for those who suffer from persecution. (For . . . )

*Silence*

Lord, in your mercy:
*Hear our prayer.*

Lord,
here is a follower of Christ
who is suffering:
she has been beaten,
tortured and thrown into jail
for standing up
for the rights
of her fellow human beings.

Lord, we pray for those who suffer to win liberation for the
oppressed. (For . . . )

*Silence*

Lord, in your mercy:
*Hear our prayer.*

## Thirteenth Sunday after Pentecost

Lord,
here is a follower of Christ
who is suffering:
his body is near to exhaustion,
his heart is near to breaking
as he feeds and tends
those dying of starvation and disease
in a famine-ridden land.

Lord, we pray for those who suffer at the plight of the world's
hungry. (For . . . )

*Silence*

Lord, in your mercy:
*Hear our prayer.*

Lord,
here is a follower of Christ
who is suffering:
she finds that the people
God has called her to love
distrust and reject her
because the colour of her skin,
her accent, her background,
are different from theirs.

Lord, we pray for those who suffer through the prejudiced attitude
of others. (For . . . )

*Silence*

Lord, in your mercy:
*Hear our prayer.*

Lord,
here is a follower of Christ
who is suffering
as he watches the person
he loves and needs
weaken and die;
as he wonders about
a God who allows
suffering and untimely death.

Lord, we pray for those who suffer because those they love are
suffering. (For . . . )

*Silence*

Lord, in your mercy:
*Hear our prayer.*

Lord,
here is a follower of Christ
who is suffering
as she watches the church
betray its calling
to suffering, redeeming love;
she sees it becoming
comfortable, apathetic,
inward-looking.

Lord, we pray for those who suffer because of the church's
deafness to the demands of love. (For . . . )

*Silence*

Lord, in your mercy:
*Hear our prayer.*

We make our prayers in the name of Christ, who did not turn his
back on the way of suffering love, but died on the cross to reveal to
us the victory of that love. *Amen.*

# Fourteenth Sunday after Pentecost
## (Trinity 13)

### The Neighbour

Jesus said,
'You shall love your neighbour
as yourself.'

Lord, we pray
that you will teach us
how to love ourselves.
We believe
that it is in loving you
that true joy and peace
are to be found.
We believe
that it is in obedience to you
that we truly love ourselves,
for you give us
what is good.

We pray
that you will make this,
your church, a place of
mutual love and care,
where, in building one another up,
we will grow
to the full stature
of the children of God;
that we may be a people
ready to meet the needs
of our neighbours
with selflessness, patience,
understanding and wisdom.

*Silence*

Lord, we pray
that you will teach us
how to forgive ourselves.
We believe
in your forgiveness:
help us to accept it
and to live by it,
to let nothing that we do
come between us
and you.
We pray
that you will make this,
your church,
a place of forgiveness,
where all find acceptance,
where wounds are healed,
so that we can find
the resources of courage
to absorb the hurt
our neighbours inflict upon us
and not to return it;
to offer them the hope
of forgiveness and new life.

*Silence*

Lord, we pray
that you will teach us
how to provide well
for our own lives;
how to spend our money
and our time
in a manner worthy
of your kingdom of love.
We pray that you will make this,
your church,
a place of generosity,
where your people give freely
of all that they have
in order to meet the needs
of their neighbours, who,
throughout the world,
are hungry, homeless,
destitute and ill.

## Fourteenth Sunday after Pentecost

*Silence*

Lord, we pray
that you will teach us
to live for
and to worship
the goodness and truth
we find in you
and so find the riches
of real life in you.
We pray that you will make this,
your church,
a place where love,
shared worship
and deep fellowship
lead to spiritual growth
so that we might be able
to take your Good News
to our neighbours, who are hungry
for peace and hope and love,
for life with a meaning.

*Silence*

Lord, may we love our neighbours as ourselves, with the love that
you have shown us in Christ Jesus. *Amen*.

# Fifteenth Sunday after Pentecost
## *(Trinity 14)*

✓

## *The Family*

L: Lord, in your mercy:
R: *Hear our prayer.*

Let us pray for families:

Lord, we pray for
the members of our own family,
the people we live with
and those who live away.
We thank you
for the love and support
that we have received
from one another.
We bring before you
the areas of tension
within our family's life:
quarrels that have not yet been resolved;
relationships that are difficult;
problems that are causing anxiety.
We pray for the members of our own family who are ill,
or sad or troubled.
We commend into your care
the children of our family
and ask that you will guide their parents
into wise and loving ways of nurture.

Lord, in your mercy:
*Hear our prayer.*

Lord, we pray
for the family of the church
and for our own church family here in . Christ Church
We thank you, and for

old and young alike,
for the fellowship and love
that we find in our life
shared together in Christ.
We bring before you
the areas of tension
within our church:
the times when the interests
of different groups conflict;
the clashes over understanding
what your gospel means;
arguments over money and property,
arguments between individuals.
We pray for those who are ill (for . . . )
who have been bereaved (for . . . )
or who are in any kind of need or anxiety (for . . . )
We pray for the children of our church, ——————— *we pray for*
for the Sunday School (Junior Church)
and for those on the Cradle Roll
and we ask that the love
and the care that we show them
may lead them into knowing
Christ as Lord and friend.

Lord, in your mercy:
*Hear our prayer.*

Lord, we pray
for family life within this nation
and for those without a family
~~in our family orientated society.~~
We pray for the elderly
and those who feel lonely
because they have lost
the people they love;
for those who live at a distance
from family and friends.
We pray for young couples
embarking on marriage,
that they may grow together
in wisdom and love.
We pray for families
where there is tension:

*quarrelling*

friction between the generations;
disharmony between parents;
stress and anxiety caused by hardship and ill-health.
We pray for the nation's children:
for those from broken homes;
for those abused and neglected;
for those made anxious
by the tension in which they live.

Lord, in your mercy:
*Hear our prayer.*

Lord, we pray
for the family of humankind
in every place.
We pray for those
who are the victims of
injustice and oppression (for . . . )
We pray for those
whose countries are at war (for . . . )
We pray for those
who are destitute and hungry (for . . . )
We pray for the children of the world,
pledging ourselves to work for their future,
that they may know a time of peace and plenty.

Lord, in your mercy:
*Hear our prayer.*

In the name of our Brother, Jesus, through whom we have become
your children, *Amen.*

# Sixteenth Sunday after Pentecost
*(Trinity 15)*

## Those in Authority ✓

L: King of kings, Lord of lords:
*R: We will serve you above all other.*

Let us pray
for those who have authority over our lives
because they wield political power;
for governments elected by the people
and those imposed upon them
by tradition or force of arms.

We pray that governments
may serve their people
with wisdom, justice and compassion.

King of kings, Lord of lords:
*We will serve you above all other.*

Let us pray
for those who have authority over our lives
~~because they have authority over us~~
at our places of work:
for all those in charge of others;
for leaders of industry and business;
for leaders of trades unions.

We pray ~~for those in charge~~
~~of the work of others,~~
that they may be fairminded,
honest and caring.

King of kings, Lord of lords:
*We will serve you above all other.*

Let us pray
for those who have authority over our lives
because they influence our ways of thinking:
for teachers and lecturers;
for journalists and broadcasters.

We pray for those who inform us
that they may strive to be
knowledgable, truthful and balanced.

King of kings, Lord of lords:
*We will serve you above all other.*

Let us pray
for those who have authority over our lives
because their love and nurturing
affects the people we become:
for parents and guardians;
for friends and partners.

We pray for those who care for us,
that they may be responsible,
loving and supportive.

King of kings, Lord of lords:
*We will serve you above all other.*

Let us pray
for those who are in positions of authority
within the life of the church:
for all ministers of the Word and sacrament;
for all preachers and teachers;
for those responsible for discussing and
formulating church doctrine, practice, and
attitudes and action.

We pray for all those with
authority within the church,
that they may serve God and his world
with humility, love and understanding.

King of kings, Lord of lords:
*We will serve you above all other.*

*Sixteenth Sunday after Pentecost*

Let us pray
for ourselves, as we try
with the help of God's Holy Spirit
to discover the right authorities for our lives,
as we search for the true morality
that is dictated by love,
as we make decisions about the ways
in which we spend ourselves and our lives.

We pray that you, Lord,
will bring your true authority
to bear upon our lives.

King of kings, Lord of lords:
*We will serve you above all other.*

In the name of our Lord and Master, Jesus Christ, *Amen.*

# Seventeenth Sunday after Pentecost
## (Trinity 16)

### The Proof of Faith

L: The Lord hears our prayer:
*R: Thanks be to God.*

Lord, in the power of your Holy Spirit
make us a people faithful to you
and faithful to humankind,
in all that we say,
in all that we do,
and in all that we are.

The Lord hears our prayer:
*Thanks be to God.*

Lord, in a world
where we are asked
to put our faith
in political systems
that promise much more
than they can deliver,
keep us faithful
to the vision of your kingdom
of love and justice,
of freedom and mercy,
that in our work together
for the peoples of the world
your concern for humankind
may be found.

Lord, in the power of your Holy Spirit,
make us a people faithful to you.

The Lord hears our prayer:
*Thanks be to God.*

## Seventeenth Sunday after Pentecost

Lord, in a world
where we all need
to put our faith
in other people, : working, relying trust them
help us to be
trustworthy and kind,
to be ready to listen
to those in trouble,
to be generous givers
to those in need;
that in our faithfulness
and our self-giving love
your faithfulness and love
may be found.

Lord, in the power of the Holy Spirit,
make us a people faithful to you.

The Lord hears our prayer:
*Thanks be to God.*

Lord, in a world
where hatred sometimes
seems more real than love,
where suffering seems constant
and joy in life fleeting,
we pray for those
whose faith in you
is being tested,
asking that they may find
proof of your love
even in hard times
and that in their courage,
their steadfastness and hope,
your resurrection power
may be found.        Lord we bring to you :

Lord, in the power of your Holy Spirit,
make us a people faithful to you.

The Lord hears our prayer:
*Thanks be to God.*

Lord, in a world
where Christians challenge people
          we

190

to put their faith in you,
we ask that your Holy Spirit
may constantly breathe life
into the words of the church,
that they may result — this
in a re-turning to you;
in actions of love;
in new vision and hope.
We pray
that every Christian,
in every place, Christ Church
may show, by a life
of courageous love,
the true meaning
of faith in you.

Lord, in the power of your Holy Spirit,
make us a people faithful to you
and faithful to humankind, others
in all that we say,
in all that we do,
and in all that we are.

The Lord hears our prayer:
*Thanks be to God.*

In the name of Jesus Christ, our faithful Lord, *Amen*.

# Eighteenth Sunday after Pentecost
*(Trinity 17)*

## The Offering of Life ✓

Lord, we bring to you
our concern about the world:
our concern for ~~the oppressed~~,
the powerless and exploited;
our concern about injustice
and about war
and we offer you
our votes and our voices,
our pens and our power,     *with you,*
our prayers.    *to make a difference –*
(We pray for . . .

*Silence*

Lord, we bring to you
our concern about the world:
our concern for ~~the needy~~,
the hungry and the homeless;
our concern about disease and want
and we offer you
our money and our time,
our standard of living,
our prayers.
(We pray for . . . )

*Silence*

Lord, we bring to you
our concern about our society:
our concern for the disadvantaged
and those discriminated against;
our concern for the young
our concern for the elderly

and we offer you
our help and our family life,
our friendship and our work,
our prayers.
(We pray for . . . )

*Silence*

Lord, we bring to you
our concern about the people
whom we know and love:
concern for those ill in body or mind;
concern for the bereaved or sorrowful;
concern for the anxious or depressed
and we offer you
our listening and our doing,
our words and our touch,
our prayers.
(We pray for . . . )

*Silence*

Lord,
in Jesus Christ we see
your concern for the world
and for each one of us
and we learn the truth,
that your name is Love.
We offer you
our adoration and thanks,
our love and our lives,
our prayers
that you will use us
and perfect us.

*Silence*

We offer you our prayers and our lives in the name of Jesus Christ,
who gave his life for us. *Amen.*

# Nineteenth Sunday after Pentecost
## *(Trinity 18)*

### *The Life of Faith*

L: The Lord hears our prayer:
*R: Thanks be to God.*

Let us make our prayers in faith,
For we know that the Spirit of God
Is at work in the world, willing
That which is good for God's creation.

I ask your prayers for the world
At a time when its future existence
Is a matter of uncertainty:
For peace between nations
And within countries;
For governments to look to long-term benefits
And not short-term expediencies;
For the proper care, education and nurturing
Of the children of the world.
(For . . . )

*Silence*

The Lord hears our prayer:
*Thanks be to God.*

I ask your prayers for the suffering of the world;
For those who have lost faith
In the love of others or of God:
For those who go hungry, who thirst
Or who are homeless;
For those who are ill, or wounded,
Or who are disabled;
For the bereaved, and those who now
Watch over a dying loved one;
For the victims of warfare, of crime

Or of persecution;
For children, whose upbringing
Has left them emotionally scarred.
(For . . . )

*Silence*

The Lord hears our prayer:
*Thanks be to God.*

Let us make our prayers in faith,
For we know that the Spirit of God
Is at work in our lives, encouraging,
Enabling and healing us.

I ask your prayers for the people
With whom we share our daily lives and work:
For those whose faith in the goodness of life
Is being tested by illness, anxiety or sorrow;
For those who feel thay have little to live for
Because they are bereaved or depressed or infirm;
For those for whom faith in a loving God
Is a problem and not a joy:
Those wrestling with feelings of doubt,
Those outraged by the suffering of the world,
Those unable to believe that they are forgiven;
For people we know who are finding life difficult
for any reason . . .

*Silence*

The Lord hears our prayer:
*Thanks be to God.*

I ask your prayers for the church,
Both here in . . . and throughout the world:
For those who are persecuted in any way
Because of the faith to which they hold;
For ministers and preachers, leaders and teachers
That they may convey
The truth of the gospel by which we can live;
For the whole church of Christ,
That she may remain faithful to her faithful Lord;
For ourselves,
For the grace to live by faith alone.
(For . . . )

## Nineteenth Sunday after Pentecost

*Silence*

The Lord hears our prayer:
*Thanks be to God.*

Heavenly Father, your love for us, which we see in Christ, is
constant and never failing. Light up our lives with faith in you, that
we, like the saints who have gone before us, may be loyal servants
and shining witnesses to your Good News for all. In Jesus' name,
*Amen.*

# Twentieth Sunday after Pentecost
*(Trinity 19)*

## *Citizens of Heaven*

Let us pray
    as citizens of heaven
    where God is Lord and King:

For the citizens of the world,
Whose rulers are human and fallible;
For countries where governments
Oppress or exploit their citizens; *people*
For countries divided by barriers
Of class, wealth, race or religion;
For countries where people suffer
The ravages of warfare or famine: —→
We pray that in the governing of their citizens *people*
The rulers of the world may govern according to
The will of the King of kings,
Who is Wisdom, Justice, Mercy and Compassion.

Let us pray
    as citizens of heaven
    ~~brothers and sisters~~
    to Christ Jesus our Lord:

For those whom we, ~~as servants~~
~~In the kingdom of God,~~
Are called to love,
That we may meet their needs
And not our own;
For those who have little status in the eyes of most,
the destitute, ~~the depraved,~~
~~the criminal,~~ the outcast;
For those whose human rights have been infringed,
The hungry, the persecuted,
the tortured, the neglected;

For those who find it hard to play a full role in society,
the handicapped, the unemployed,
the lonely, the housebound;
For all those we know who are ill or anxious or sad . . .
For the bereaved and dying,
Facing the reality of the boundary between life and death. *We equally*
We pray that we may show that in God's kingdom *pastor*
There is comfort and healing,
Acceptance and hope,
And abundant life for all.

Let us pray
    as citizens of heaven
    ~~whose lives~~ are ruled
    by God's Holy Spirit:

For the church, that her members may ~~be~~ *develop a clear vision*
~~The people of the Kingdom of God,~~ *for of direction and follow it*
~~Remaining loyal to their vision of God~~
Through all the difficulties and compromises of life;
For the institutions and committees of the church,
That they might retain proper priorities,
Patience, wisdom and love;
For ourselves, that we may
Take up our Christian responsibilities
With enthusiasm and in faith.

We pray that the work and witness of the citizens of heaven, *that we*
~~Christians past and present~~, may speed the coming of the Kingdom
of God upon earth. In the name of Jesus Christ our Lord, *Amen*.

# Twenty-first Sunday after Pentecost
*(Trinity 20)*

## *Endurance*

'I believe in this cause – but my belief is beginning to buckle under the strain. Will we ever see the end for which we struggle? Will it have been worth the cost?'

Heavenly Father, we pray that you will give courage, wisdom and patience to all those who work to improve the lot of their fellow human beings, in the face of hard, uncaring or unjust leaders. May they cling to their vision of a just and caring society, a vision for which they live or are prepared to die.

' "The poor will always be with you" – that saying tears me apart. I have given money, time, myself; fed one child to see two die. My care seems to be only a drop of love in an ocean of suffering.'

Heavenly Father, we pray that you will give courage, energy and the support of your Comforter to all those who care for the hungry, the diseased and the destitute, in the face of their own feelings of powerlessness and pain. May they find signs of hope and reasons for joy in their work, even in the midst of sorrow and suffering.

'I felt that it was right, for me, to nurse her myself. Home is where she wants to be, with those who know and love her best. But I'm at the end of my strength, my patience, my humour. I just don't know how to carry on.'

Heavenly Father, we pray that you will give courage and strength to all those who care for people they love who are sick or dying. We pray for any we know who are finding life a struggle because of their own illness or that of others. May they be aware of our concern for them and of your loving care.

> 'I was overjoyed when I realized that being a Christian means having a new start. But now I'm not so sure it makes me happy. Accepting God's forgiveness means I have to take responsibility for trying to live a Christian life. And that is hard, an uphill climb. I sometimes feel I'd rather slip back completely than carry on toiling up the mountain in the hope of reaching the top.'

Heavenly Father, we ask that you will give each one of us courage, endurance and the will to persevere as we try to live truly Christian lives. In your Son, Jesus Christ, you have shown us that you are ready to forgive whenever we fall short of your mark for us. Give us the help of your Holy Spirit, the Lord and Giver of Life, that we may have the strength to endure all, as Christians, now and until the end of our lives. May we find peace in our struggling, joy in our fellowship, hope in our perseverance and the love that never lets go.

In the name of Jesus Christ, who endured to the end that we might know the love that is at the heart of all creation, *Amen*.

# Watchnight

Who will watch
for the coming of Christ?
Who will see in this New Year?
Who will watch with us?

I am awake,
unable to sleep
for hunger, for anxiety
about what tomorrow
will bring for me
and for my family.
I await your coming, Lord,
as bread for our mouths,
medicine for our sickness.
As this New Year comes I watch
for a future for my children.

*Silence*

Who will watch with us?

I am awake,
for the light in my cell
is never turned low
and fear of torture
constricts my heart.
I await your coming, Lord,
as freedom for the oppressed,
justice for the exploited.
As the New Year comes I watch
for a future for my people.

*Silence*

## Watchnight

**Who will watch with us?**

I am awake
as I sit by the side
of a friend who is dying
and listen to the last sounds
of the life of one I love.
I await your coming, Lord,
as death to heal such suffering,
as a comforting hand on my arm.
As the New Year comes I watch
for a future beyond death.

*Silence*

**Who will watch with us?**

I am awake,
the thoughts in my head
allow me no rest,
I am filled with guilt,
fear, anxiety, regret.
I await your coming, Lord,
as the knowledge of forgiveness,
as courage, peace and hope.
As the New Year comes I watch
for a future new beginning.

*Silence*

We watch
for the coming of Christ.
We see in the New Year.
We watch together.

We are awake,
celebrating in worship,
alert with love,
ready for service,
open to God.
We await your coming, Lord,
as Life for the world,
as joy and love, hope and peace.
As the New Year comes we watch
for the coming of your new kingdom.

202

*Silence*

Lord, knock on the door of our lives,
for we are ready to open to you,
to your brothers and sisters in need,
to the whole of your world.

In the name of Jesus Christ, *Amen.*

# Aldersgate Sunday

L: Lord, in your mercy:
*R: Hear our prayer.*

Let us pray for the world
named by John Wesley as his parish:

Lord, we pray
for those with power
within the world,
that in the exercise
of their power over others
they may be ruled
not only by their heads
but by loving hearts:
that wisdom may be informed by compassion;
that justice may be tempered with mercy;
that policies may be determined by human need.

Lord, in your mercy:
*Hear our prayer.*

Let us pray for all humankind
for whom we believe Christ died:

Lord, we pray
for the peoples of the world.
We bring to you
our concern for those who suffer:
the persecuted and oppressed;
the hungry and destitute;
the victims of warfare;
the sick and the injured;
the dying and the bereaved
and we ask that you

will fill our hearts with such love
that we may work with you
to bring the love and peace
of your reign
into this suffering world.

Lord, in your mercy:
*Hear our prayer.*

Let us pray for those who,
like John Wesley,
seek a deeper relationship of faith with God:

Lord, we pray for those
who seek to know
and to love you better:
for those looking
for a purpose in life
and those who feel attracted
to the Christian faith;
for those assailed by doubts
about your existence
or the power of your love;
for those who doubt
their own commitment
or their own claim
to be your followers;
for the newly born babes in Christ
and for mature Christians
facing new challenges;
for those who feel their faith
is too much of the mind
or too much of the heart;
for all Christians, everywhere,
as they strive towards
the perfection of love
in union with Christ.

Lord, in your mercy:
*Hear our prayer.*

Let us pray for the Methodist Church
founded by John Wesley.

## Aldersgate Sunday

Lord, we pray
for the Methodist Church
throughout the world,
that it may remain faithful
to its calling to bring
salvation and love
to those it serves.
We pray
for the Methodist Church
in this land:
for its ministers, leaders and preachers
and for congregations
in city, town or village.
We pray for the congregation here in . . .
that we may be united
by our faith in you
and our service to the people
among whom we live and work.

Lord, in your mercy:
*Hear our prayer.*

In the name of Jesus Christ, our Lord and Master, *Amen.*

# All Saint's Day

L: Lord, in your mercy:
R: *Hear our prayer*.

We are members of the household of faith,
Members of the communion of saints
Which is of the past, the present and the future
And which is found throughout the world.

Let us pray:
Heavenly Father, we remember before you, with thanks,
the lives of those Christians who have gone before us:
the great leaders and thinkers of the church,
and those whose goodness transformed all they touched;
those who died as martyrs for their faith
and those who lived only for their Lord.
We remember those who have died
who had a great influence on our Christian lives
through preaching, teaching, nurture or care.
Lord, we ask that through your Holy Spirit
you will give us the grace to follow the example
of those who, in past ages, have been faithful to you
and worked hard for the coming of your kingdom.
May we receive from them
insight and inspiration for the present,
vision, hope and courage for the future.
Building upon their achievements
and learning from their mistakes,
may we, with them, be co-workers with you
in the fulfilling of your plan of redemption
for the whole created world.

Lord, in your mercy:
*Hear our prayer.*

Heavenly Father, we remember before you, by name,
those from this congregation who have recently died . . .
We give thanks to you for their lives and example
and for all that they have meant to us.
We pray for those who grieve for them,
that they may be sustained by the knowledge
that death cannot separate us from your love
and that we are all one in the life
of our Risen Lord and Saviour, Jesus Christ.

Lord, in your mercy:
*Hear our prayer.*

Heavenly Father, we remember before you
the communion of saints of this present age.
We celebrate our unity and fellowship
with Christians throughout the world
and pray that our unity might show itself
in love and concern, generous deeds and courageous action.
We pray for those saints who are hungry and destitute,
who are oppressed, reviled and persecuted,
who are unable to preach and teach your gospel.
We pray for those from this congregation
who are ill, or bereaved, or anxious,
for . . .
that they may know your healing presence and love.
Lord, we ask that through your Holy Spirit
you will deepen the unity of the church,
that we may be your one, holy people,
set aside by you, a beacon of shining love
to all the world.

Lord, in your mercy:
*Hear our prayer.*

Heavenly Father, we remember before you
the newest generation of your saints
and we pray for the future of the church
and for those Christians who are yet to come.
We pray for all those who are responsible
for the Christian nurture and upbringing of the young
and we remember before you those recently baptized

and welcomed into the membership of this church . . .
Lord, we ask that through your Holy Spirit
the church may remain faithful to you
through every future change and challenge.
We pray that this congregation
may be a community of truth and love
where faith can flourish and grow.
We look forward to the coming of your kingdom
when we, with Christians not yet born
and the saints and witnesses of the past,
may together praise you and rejoice
in the final triumph of your perfect Love.

Lord, in your mercy
*Hear our prayer.*

In the name of Jesus Christ,
the Lord and Saviour of us all, *Amen.*

# Remembrance Sunday

On this Remembrance Sunday
we remember past wars:
those who have fought in them;
those who have lived through them;
those who have died in them.

*Silence*

On this Remembrance Sunday
we pray for the peace of the world.
We remember before God
areas where there is armed conflict:
we pray for . . .
We remember before God
all those who actively work for peace,
and pray for . . .
and for the United Nations' Organization.
In the name of the Prince of Peace
we pray for peace.

*Silence*

On this Remembrance Sunday
we pray for the victims of past wars.
We remember before God
those who died in battle,
those who died from the consequences
of injury or disease.
We remember before God
those permanently maimed or disabled,
those psychologically scarred or disturbed.
We remember before God
those civilians killed by enemy action,
those who died at our country's hands.

We remember before God
those bereaved by the wars,
those who still cope with war's consequences.
In the name of our Lord Jesus Christ
who rose triumphant
over suffering and death
we pray for an end
to the suffering of war.

*Silence*

On this Remembrance Sunday
we pray for the victims of current conflicts.
We remember before God
young boys trained to fight,
young children trained to hate.
We remember before God
families turned into homeless refugees,
families deprived of father or mother.
We remember before God
those blinded or maimed,
those driven insane.
We remember before God
lands split by civil war,
land laid waste and made barren.
In the name of him
who taught us to love
even our enemies
we pray for an end
to the destructive hatred of war.

*Silence*

On this Remembrance Sunday
we pray for the future of our world
threatened by nuclear destruction
and we remember
that God has called us to work together
for his kingdom of love and of peace.
We pray that he will equip us for the task
and we look forward to that time
when God's love will triumph finally
over hatred and greed and death.

We make our prayers in the name of our Risen Lord, Jesus Christ.
*Amen.*

# Overseas Mission

L: Living Lord, Light of the World:
R: *Let your love shine in every land.*

Lord, we pray
for those who go out from our country
as missionaries overseas:
to minister to the churches
and to share their expertise
in medicine, education,
agriculture, engineering
or administration.
We pray
for those in training at college,
those just starting work,
those established in their posts;
for their partners,
for the family they take with them
and those they leave behind.
(For . . . )

Living Lord, Light of the World:
*Let your love shine in every land.*

Lord, we pray
for those who go out from our country
as missionaries overseas,
that you will fill them with your Holy Spirit,
who gives courage and wisdom
to those facing new ways of life
and new ways of thinking;
who binds the church together
so that Christians in every place
share in a common life.

We pray
that all who go as missionaries
may serve their fellow human beings
with humility and understanding,
with imagination and love.
We pray
for those finding life on the mission field
hard or frustrating,
those who are lonely or afraid
and those overwhelmed by their situation.
We ask that you, Lord, will be with them
and show them the way ahead.

Living Lord, Light of the World:
*Let your love shine in every land.*

Lord, we pray
for the work of those who are missionaries overseas,
that they may be effective messengers
of your self-giving love for humankind.
We pray that through them you will:
    feed the hungry;
    teach young and old;
    heal the sick;
    bring sight to the blind
    and good news to all.
We pray that in the fight with poverty,
disease, ignorance and death,
God's love may triumph
with Resurrection power,
as missionaries and people work together
with hope and determination.

Living Lord, Light of the World:
*Let your love shine in every land.*

Lord, we pray
for those in this country
who support the work of missionaries overseas,
for those who raise money and offer prayers
and for those engaged in specific projects.
(For . . . )
We pray
for the work of this congregation,

for . . .
for all who collect and donate money
for Overseas Mission (and the JMA),
for the Overseas Mission (and JMA)
secretaries and treasurers . . .
We pray
for the work of the Overseas Division
in its organization and pastoral care
of Methodist missionaries overseas.

Living Lord, Light of the World:
*Let your love shine in every land.*

Lord, we pray
that we may be made more aware
of our unity with fellow Christians
in every land and of every race.
We pray
that you will make us receptive
to what we can learn about you
from churches in other lands
and with other cultures.
We pray
that we may learn from our past mistakes
and discover new and exciting
possibilities for missionary work.
We pray
for those who have come from overseas
as missionaries to this land,
that we may be open and welcoming
to them, their families and their word.
(For . . . )

Living Lord, Light of the World:
*Let your love shine in every land.*

Lord God,
you are the Father Creator
of the whole world,
of every man, woman and child.
We pray
that the family of humankind
may become one
in your love.

In the name of Christ,
who gave himself for us all, *Amen*.

# Harvest Thanksgiving

L: Lord, make us co-workers with you:
*R: That humankind may reap a full harvest.*

Lord, we pray
for this world you have given us:
for the soil in which we plant our seeds;
for the pasture on which we graze our animals;
for the mineral resources that fuel our industries;
for the seas and rivers where we fish.
Lord,
teach us how to treat your world
with the respect it needs and deserves;
teach us to observe
the rhythms and balance of nature;
teach us to conserve
the earth's riches and resources
that there may be a harvest-time
for generations to come.

Lord, make us co-workers with you:
*That humankind may reap a full harvest.*

Lord, we pray
for this world you have given us:
for the planting of seeds;
for the propagation of stock and fish;
for mining and drilling;
for the birth of new ideas.
We remember before you, Lord;
those who cannot plant
because hunger has driven them
to eat the seed;
those whose animals are diseased and dying;

those whose seas and rivers have been over-fished;
those whose mineral resources
are on the verge of running out.
Lord,
teach us to understand
your world as an entirety
that new beginnings may come
from sharing and planning together.

Lord, make us co-workers with you:
*That humankind may reap a full harvest.*

Lord, we pray
for this world you have given us:
for the growing and the tending of plants;
for the husbandry of animals;
for manufacturing and service industries.
We remember before you, Lord:
lands where there is too little rain
or where the sun fails to shine;
lands where farming is inefficient
and crops and livestock fail to thrive;
industries where employees are misused or exploited
or where strife and tension stop or hamper the work.
Lord,
teach us to make the most of your world,
to make allowances for its imperfections,
to acknowledge the needs and rights
of our fellow human beings.

Lord, make us co-workers with you:
*That humankind may reap a full harvest.*

Lord, we pray
for this world you have given us:
for the harvest time
    of plant crops
    of livestock
    of the seas
    of minerals
    of industry
    of the arts
and we pray for all those whose harvests have failed,
remembering especially . . .

### Harvest Thanksgiving

Lord,
teach us to give as well as to take,
to use what you have given us wisely and well,
to see that we do not benefit
from the hardship of others,
to share all that we have
with others who are without.

Lord, make us co-workers with you:
*That humankind may reap a full harvest.*

In the name of Jesus Christ
who came to bring to ripeness
the Harvest of God. *Amen.*

# Christian Citizenship Sunday

The Law of the Kingdom of God:
You shall love the Lord your God
With all your heart and mind and soul
And your neighbour as yourself.

L: Lord, as the people of God we pray:
R: *Help us to keep your rule of love.*

Who is my neighbour?
My neighbour lives with me.
She is a member of my family.
She needs me, even if we
Sometimes hurt each other.
I know her well:
Her fears and habits;
Her talents and ambitions.
I hold her in my mind.

*Silence*

Lord, as the people of God we pray:
*Help us to keep your rule of love.*

Who is my neighbour?
I meet him every day
At work or at school.
Sometimes he is a friend
And sometimes not.
He needs me, even if
He keeps himself apart.
He has problems and worries
And needs to confide.

He needs to feel liked
And respected.
I hold him in my mind.

*Silence*

Lord, as the people of God we pray:
*Help us to keep your rule of love.*

Who is my neighbour?
She lives next door to me
But only feels really at home
When the family are all around her.
We find it hard to talk,
Because her English is so poor;
But she needs me
To show her that life
Beyond her front door
Is not totally hostile.
I hold her in my mind.

*Silence*

Lord, as the people of God we pray:
*Help us to keep your rule of love.*

Who is my neighbour?
He lives hundreds of miles away
And I shall never meet him;
But I caught a glimpse of his face
On the television last night.
He is very small
But his hunger is very great.
He needs me
To do what I can
To get food to him;
To try to change the world
In which he dies.
I hold him in my mind.

*Silence*

Lord, as the people of God we pray:
*Help us to keep your rule of love.*

Who are my neighbours?
They are sitting in the pews around me,
Praying as I pray,
Breathing the same air,
Sharing the same Spirit.
I need them
To help me make my life
And so that we can
Together serve the world.
I need them
To accept the love
I need to give.
I hold them in my mind.

*Silence*

Lord, as the people of God we pray:
*Help us to keep your rule of love.*

In Jesus' name, *Amen.*

# Church Anniversary

L: Lord, this is our prayer:
R: *Help us to know and to do your will.*

On this Church Anniversary Sunday, let us pray for the church here in . . . :
that the Holy Spirit may inspire us to worship and lead us into deeper fellowship;
that we may continue to pass on the teachings of our faith and our traditions of service to succeeding generations;
that we may strive to serve the community within which we live with commitment, vision and enthusiasm;
that within our fellowship there may be found comfort for the sorrowful, strength for the anxious, compassion for the sick and concern and love for all.

Lord, this is our prayer:
*Help us to know and to do your will.*

Let us pray
for the minister (and his/her wife/husband [and family])
that he/she may find the resources of faith that can equip him/her for his/her tasks
and that they may be upheld by our care and prayers for them;
for Sunday School (Junior Church) teachers and youth group leaders, that they may, by their words and personality, impress upon those they teach the truth and joys of the Christian life;
for those who hold positions of responsibility in our church,
those who act as pastors to us, and on our behalf,
those who are stewards of our property and finance,
that all may fulfil their calling eagerly, conscientiously, and with imagination.

Lord, this is our prayer:
*Help us to know and to do your will.*

Let us pray
for the whole church of God,
for the breaking down
of the barriers between believers,
so that we might go forward
in unity of service
to our one Lord and Master.
(We pray for ecumenical work in this area . . . )

Let us pray
for the community which we,
with Christians from other churches,
are called to serve;
for the areas of need within it;
(For . . . or *silence*)

Let us pray
for our country, for which we have many responsibilities;
for the areas of need within it;
(For . . . or *silence*)

Let us pray
for the world which we are charged to change;
for the areas of need within it;
(For . . . or *silence*)

Lord, may we, your church, find the right ways of helping your
needy children throughout the world.

Lord, this is our prayer:
*Help us to know and to do your will.*

Let us pray
for those who belong to our church family,
for those who are ill, at home or in hospital;
(for . . . or *silence*)
for those who are housebound or unable to get to church;
(for . . . or *silence*)
for those who are bereaved or face losing someone they love;
(for . . . or *silence*)
for those who are worried or depressed;
(for . . . or *silence*)

for those who have moved away from this church in the past year;
(for . . . or *silence*)
for those who no longer come to church,
that they may be drawn back into our fellowship.

Lord, this is our prayer:
*Help us to know and to do your will.*

Lord, we give thanks to you for the lives of your faithful servants
in every age and for the lives of the members of this community of
faith who have been witnesses to your love. (We remember
especially . . . )

Lord, we, with them, are the living stones with which you build
your church. We pray that we too may remain faithful to our
calling, as did your Son, Jesus, that by our steadiness in your Holy
Spirit, our lives may be the examples upon which those after us
may build. *Amen.*